LITTLE BOOK OF
EVENTING

LITTLE BOOK OF
EVENTING

First published in the UK in 2013

© G2 Entertainment Limited 2013

www.G2ent.co.uk

Printed and bound in Europe

ISBN 978-1-782811-99-2

The views in this book are those of the author but they are general views only and readers are urged to consult the relevant and qualified specialist for individual advice in particular situations.
G2 Entertainment Limited hereby exclude all liability to the extent permitted by law of any errors or omissions in this book and for any loss, damage or expense (whether direct or indirect) suffered by a third party relying on any information contained in this book.

Contents

Introduction

The *Little Book of Eventing* will take the reader through the history, development, scope and opportunities in what, at the highest level, has been an Olympic sport since 1912. Eventing involves riding horses and is enjoyed by both adults and children, male and female, in an increasing number of countries around the world.

The term, when typed, always throws up the spell check, which is perhaps unsurprising, since the term in no way describes the activity. It doesn't help that in its ever evolving history, it has been named many things, and undergone many formats.

This book aims to be an introduction to the uninitiated, a history for participants right up to Olympic level who may be unaware of the roots of the sport they love, and a guide to those who may have high or modest competitive ambitions, or just want to be part of an outdoor pastime, which still relies on a vast number of volunteers at all levels to make it happen. Likewise, spectators who come to watch at the bigger events will increase their enjoyment with a little more knowledge.

As in all sports, Eventing has thrown up its stars over the years, both human and equine, and this *Little Book* will introduce the reader to many of these.

As will become apparent to the reader very soon, Great Britain, first with the first Badminton, and then the network of events that have followed over the years, swiftly became the world centre of the sport, so the book, almost by definition, is very British based, though I hope unbiased. Britain hasn't won an Olympic team Eventing gold since 1972, though they have done well at European and World Championships. Both the USA and Canada have had triumphs, as have some continental competitors, but it is those from Australia and New Zealand who have had the greatest outside impact over the years, either coming on raiding parties or basing themselves in the UK.

What is Eventing?

Eventing is the test of all-round horsemanship, made up, today, of three distinct elements: Dressage, a subjectively judged, compulsory test of ridden movements in an arena; Cross Country, a jumping test over several thousand metres, involving up to 30 solid, natural obstacles, which must be cleared without refusal or fall in a set time, and Jumping, a round of about a dozen knock down coloured obstacles in an arena. The scoring is penalty based and the horse and rider with the lowest score, is the winner. Horse and rider must complete all phases as a combination. Men and women compete on equal terms.

Its history, however, owes everything to the training of male, military officers and their chargers. Equitation as an art spans several thousand years and, from the beginning, the soldier has used this art for his own needs. The military horse needed to be fast and tough, obedient and agile. In pursuit or retreat, speed was required to catch or avoid the enemy, on forced marches, endurance was needed to cover difficult terrain over long distances, and in close quarter fighting, obedience and agility were essential for survival. Underlying these requirements were the fundamental ones, soundness and condition. Lose your horse and you were relegated to the more exhausting ranks of the common foot soldier.

To provide a keener edge in

Above: *Army Tests*

peacetime, training competitions were devised, in which the necessary cavalry skills were put to the test. It is in these tests that Eventing has its origins; until recently many European nations still referred to the sport as 'The Military'. The format of most of these early tests is lost to history but Lt. Col. C.E.G. Hope gives some examples in his 1969 book *The Horse Trials Story*. He dates his research right back to Xenophon, who wrote in 365 BC, 'As there will, doubtless, be times when the horse will need to race downhill and uphill and on

WHAT IS EVENTING?

Right: *Pony Club*

sloping ground; times also, when he will need to leap across an obstacle, or take a flying leap from off a bank, or jump down from a height, the rider must teach and train himself and his horse to meet all emergencies. In this way the two will have a chance of saving each other.' This could be the description of the skills needed to ride round one of the great events, such as Badminton or Burghley. Much of this history is also included in *Little Book of Badminton*, as it will be explained later that Badminton is the ultimate competition in the entire sport.

The sport has distilled itself into the three phases mentioned, because each one reflects a different aspect of the training test. The Dressage tests basic obedience and control. At the more esoteric 'High School' level, not required in Eventing, some of the movements, still performed by the Lippizaners of the famous Spanish Riding School in Vienna, such as the Courbette, a flying leap with a kick back to knock an opponent off his horse or the defensive Levade, when the horse stands on its hind legs, had practical battle uses.

The Cross Country tested braveness and mutual trust of horse and rider, and the final Jumping phase was to reflect the horsemanship required to keep the horse sound after the heroics of battle day.

Cavalry Schools had their manuals, and one from the Cavalry of King Charles XI of Sweden in 1688 helpfully suggested, "When jumping a fence the rider will grab the mane, close his eyes and shout, 'Hey'."

There are reports of some other tests in the nineteenth century of 'Complete Cavalry Charger' competitions. Mainly these were straightforward long distance endurance rides, ridden collectively by the officers, covering distances of anything from 25 to 370 kilometres. Sometimes military tactics were involved towards the end of such a ride. For the US Army these competitions were, according to General Tupper Cole, "A military event based on the duty of the officer courier who got through or died."

Though the sport now consists mainly of truncated one-day versions of the all-round test, with the Cross Country, oddly running last, the original concept was a several day affair and remains the ultimate level of the sport in the format of the Three Day Event.

The French ran the first recognisable

version of this concept. The 1902 Championnat du Cheval d'Armes was put on for officers. On the Dressage day after some compulsory figures, riders could earn more points by showing off in a freestyle. Some took to performing tricks like cantering backwards, spinning on the back legs, on the spot trotting and backwards Spanish Walk. The next day there was a 4,000m Steeplechase ridden by four competitors at a time, with a speed requirement of 450m per minute, and this was followed by an Endurance section of Roads and Tracks which was 50km long. On the third day the Show Jumping, which was designed to make the competitors known to the public, was held in the Grand Palais in Paris before a large crowd.

This event was considered a great success and it became an annual affair with the intention of helping to improve the quality of riding throughout France in the tradition of hardiness, good training and style of the army, in developing equestrian tact and finesse, and increasing the experience of men and horses. Certain modifications were brought into the format. The Dressage freestyle was abolished; horses were to be examined after each phase and given

points for condition and the Steeplechase was run singly and immediately after the Roads and Tracks. A Cross Country course was included much later in 1922, and civilians and females were allowed to enter.

Meanwhile, in the early 1900s, other countries, including Sweden, Belgium and Great Britain – under the auspices of the Indian Army School of Equitation in Sangor Central Provinces – had been developing similar competitions. The British efforts were concentrated in India, as officers back home devoted their extracurricular equestrian activities to the hunting field and polo pitch. In India the expressed object was to, "encourage young officers to buy and train horses of the right stamp." The Swiss called their competition, *Gebrauchspferdeprufungen*, which can be roughly described as 'Trials for all-round horses.'

1912 turned out to be a seminal year for the future of these cavalry tests. Count Clarence von Rosen, Master of Horse to the King of Sweden at the time, promoted the idea of introducing equestrian events to the modern Olympic Games, which had been revived by Baron Guy de Coubertin in 1896. They had been proposed for London 1908,

WHAT IS EVENTING?

Right: Map of the Grafton Hunter Trial

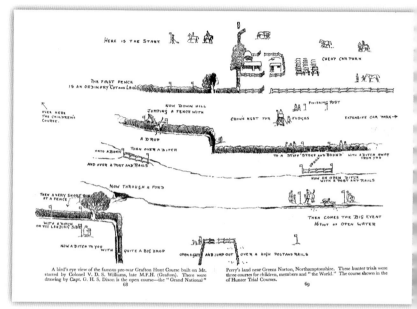

A bird's eye view of the famous pre-war Grafton Hunt Course built on Mr. started by Colonel V. D. S. Williams, late M.F.H. (Grafton). There were drawing by Capt. G. H. S. Dixon is the open course—the "Grand National" 68

Perry's land near Greens Norton, Northamptonshire. These hunter trials were three courses for children, members and "the World." The course shown in the of Hunter Trial Courses. 69

but never materialised.

The only horses that had appeared in the original Olympics, which ran from 776 BC to 393 AD, had been pulling chariots. Now the idea was to stimulate among civilians, as well as the army, an interest in equitation and to promote better standards of horsemanship. Eventing was included as a 'Pentathlon on Horseback'. The format would keep evolving, but at that first Games, as the name would suggest, it was divided into five phases over four days. It ran like this: Saturday – Roads and Tracks Endurance (50km), Cross Country (5km); Monday – Steeplechase (3km); Tuesday – Show Jumping; Wednesday – Dressage.

The Olympics returned after the First World War at the Antwerp Games in 1920. There was no Dressage, but two Endurance sections. On the first day there was 45km Roads and Tracks

followed by 5km Cross Country and a day off. After that was a 20km Roads and Tracks to a 4km Steeplechase with another day off and on the last day Show Jumping.

By Paris in 1924 the more logical order of Dressage, Endurance with Cross Country, and finally Jumping was established, but there were still days off between phases. The number of entries filled two days of Dressage and in 1928

at Amsterdam the bye days went. The Three Day Event was there, albeit lasting four days!

The scoring system is in a state of continuous flux, but the record penalty achieved by a Czech rider, Lt. Otomar Bures and Mirko, at the Berlin Olympics in 1936, will take some beating. He completed with a penalty score of 18,130.7.

With Olympic competition to

train for, trials were soon introduced to all the interested countries. At the start were Sweden, Germany, USA, France, Belgium, Denmark and Great Britain. Britain, the hunting centre of the world, normally fielded a team that was seldom disgraced, but its concept of Dressage was somewhat different to that of the European teams. 'The prevalent notion of the continental horseman was somebody who spent his time bumming around the arena, teasing his horse.' (Hope)

In 1948 the British team managers recruited two German instructors, who had been prisoners of war, to rectify the situation. The new methods took some time to sink in, due to the influence of weekend house parties and suspicion of foreign ways. When they did, however, the old methods of the Army Cavalry School at Weedon were dutifully relegated.

1948 proved significant for another reason, destined to have a much greater impact on the whole sport of Eventing. The post-war Olympic Games were hosted by London and the equestrian competitions were centred on the adjacent army towns of Sandhurst and Aldershot. There was a Three Day Event,

and it was hoped that Great Britain could do better than their team bronze at the 1936 Berlin Games, on home territory. Sadly, a medal didn't materialise for Great Britain, but watching the competition was the 10th Duke of Beaufort, who suggested to his good friend Col. Trevor Horn that a similar event at his park in Gloucestershire might give the British riders some practice before the next Olympics.

With the blessing and administrative help from the British Horse Society the first Badminton Horse Trials, hosted by the Duke and organised by Trevor Horn, was staged from 20th to 22nd April in 1949.

Few people – except some servicemen and a small number of civilian riders who had looked further afield than the usual type of English riding of hunting, racing and polo – had the slightest idea what it was all about. Dressage was certainly seen as a dark art.

That first Badminton, bravely advertising itself as "The Greatest Horse Event in Great Britain", received entries from 36 male riders, half military, half civilian, and 11 lady riders. There was a special prize for any woman completing the event. Of the 22 competitors who

Above: *Dressage High School*

started the event, eight failed to get past the Cross Country phase, including the valiant Brigadier J. Scott-Coburn who was "three times winner of the Kadir Cup, the pig sticking blue riband of India." The only lady rider to complete was Vivien Machin-Goodall, who came fifth with Neptune. The first winner was John Shedden on Golden Willow.

Badminton was an instant success and word spread about this 'new' equestrian sport. In three years the crowd had grown from a respectable first gate of 6,000 to 55,000. It now has three times that many visitors.

Some of the riders even began to

realise that good Dressage training could help in the other phases. Nevertheless it was apparent after the first event that one big Three Day Event in a year wasn't really enough. Badminton was big, complicated and expensive to run, and it was realised that something simpler and cheaper, yet combining all the elements, had to be devised. Badminton was, as it were, the apex of a new sport without any foundation. The answer was the One Day Event.

Badminton's second winner, Tony Collings – a professional riding trainer from Porlock – and Neil Gardiner from Great Auclum in Berkshire, worked out some draft rules and submitted a plan to the British Horse Society towards the end of 1949. The BHS wouldn't underwrite the event that Gardiner proposed to stage under the auspices of the South Berks Hunt, so it was Henry Wynmalen who staged the first public One Day Event in Britain on 29th March 1950 at Wellesbourne, Warwickshire.

The objects, as stated in the programme, were to "provide prospective Badminton competitors with an opportunity to practise in public over a much easier and shorter course, combined with practice in public of the Badminton Dressage test." And also to, "encourage other riders to try their hand at this most comprehensive type of riding test, where ability to cross a country and ability to produce a well trained horse count equally." That year there was no Jumping phase, only Dressage, a Roads and Tracks section and a one and a half mile Cross Country course.

These were the foundations on which the sport grew. Because of the Badminton effect the network of smaller events grew, and Britain became the epicentre of the worldwide sport. Events and venues come and go but at the time of writing there are 175 fixtures in the British calendar.

Image and How Other See the Sport

Eventing has never been afraid of its upmarket image. Indeed, it is the blue chip associations that have attracted high end sponsors. Naturally, four-wheel drive car manufacturers have featured a lot, with Mitsubishi and Land Rover long time backers of Badminton and Burghley. Toyota, Nissan, Ford, Audi and VW have all had a presence. Rolex and HSBC sponsor on an international scale.

All of the major events in Britain, and quite a lot of the smaller ones, are run in parks surrounding stately homes: Badminton, Burghley, Blenheim, Blair, Chatsworth, Bramham, Gatcombe, Belton, Firle, Weston and Houghton to name but some. In the Dressage phase at top level the riders wear top hats and tail coats. The Queen attended Badminton for many years and both Princess Anne and now her daughter, Zara Phillips, have competed at the highest level. In its early days the programmes included a plethora of hyphenated names.

Conolly-Carew, Hely-Hutchinson, Martin-Bird, Naylor-Leyland, Ross-Taylor, Cabel-Manners, Machin-Goodall, Wickham-Musgrave, Gordon-Watson, Graham-Young, Lawson-Baker, Dobson-Seaton, Fox-Pitt, Wright-Gibbins, Marsh-Smith, Spencer-Cox, Cox-Cox, Fleming-Williams, Holderness-Roddam, Prior-Palmer, Thomson-Jones, Loriston-Clarke, Fetherstone-Godley, Lindsey-Renton, Drummond-Hay, Knox-Thompson, Scott-

Cockburn, Heathcote-Amory, Freeman-Jackson, Cameron-Hayes, Blixen-Finecke, Greville Williams, Harms-Cooke, Graham-Menzies, Graham-Clark, Smith-Bingham, Mounsey-Heysham, Durston-Smith, Jobling-Purser, Kozuba-Kozubska, Smith-Flagg, Powell-Harris, Seymour-Smith, Morgan-Giles, Reeves-Smith, Marsh-Smith, Handley-Packham; Etherington-Smith; Roger-Smith; Vaughn-Jones.

There is a good 50 above, and fun to note that quite a few are hyphenated Smiths. However, two deserve special mention. In a world of army misogyny, Roosmale-Cocq passes muster, and at a time when lady riders were referred to in the continental press as 'Les Amazons', who should stand up to be counted other than a Miss Manley-Walker?

None of these names are Made-Up.

Private Eye magazine's fictitious poet, E Jarvis-Thribb, celebrated Jane Holderness-Roddam's 1978 Badminton win with his misspelled 'thribbute':

Above: *Bowler hats denote officialdom*

"So
Congratulations then
June Holderness-Roddam.

You have won.

Lucinda Prior-
Palmer was
Second.

Holderness-Roddam,
Prior-Palmer.

Both
Double barrelled.

Jarvis-Thribb
Another name
Hyphenated.

But somehow
I do not think
I will ever

Compete
At Badminton."

A BRYAN FORBES FILM

O'NEAL PLUMMER HOPKINS NEWMAN

INTERNATIONAL VELVET

Above:
International Velvet

Far Right: *A scene from the movie International Velvet*

by a quirk of birth, an act of God, have been blessed with, and view as their due, the long weekend."

He continued. "In fact if you wish to event for Britain, it would be best to pack in any job you have and ride off into the sunset in search of a private income. It's not exactly a sport for all." He does concede however that the sport attracts the brave, "...and hairy it be, and you have to take your hat off to those who do it."

By the mid-Eighties most of the hyphens had gone (though Fox-Pitt junior is at the pinnacle of the sport), and the roll call of participants less patrician and, indeed, positively democratic. This was demonstrable when the blameless Sharon Lemon won Bramham in the Eighties. Subsequently there has been another Sharon, a Gary and, indeed, a Zara in the British squad. Despite all, the image is still unashamedly upmarket.

Equestrian jargon can also seem impenetrable and excluding. Again, it was *Private Eye*, this time in the guise of their romance writer, Sylvie Krin, who spoofed this so well in the tale of Princess Anne's courting of Mark Phillips, "...and then he was off! He took

The late humourist, Willie Rushton, observed dryly in his late Seventies book, *Pigsticking, a Gentleman's Guide to Sporting Pastimes*, "The Three Day Event, as its name suggests, is designed for those who,

the first fence in his stride and cantered down to the Three Bar Gate. Up and over! With Mark scarcely touching him with his jagger whip, Rebozo vaulted majestically over the gate. Then 'The Short One' where so many lesser riders had caught their shockles on the horizontal yangling posts."

Is that any less incomprehensible than real terms such as: martingale, kimblewick, numnah, half pass, flying change, skinny and spun?

The sport, expensive, and therefore still exclusive – if not as socially as it may once have been – has many things in its favour. Men and women compete on equal terms. Empathy with an animal is essential. Both physical bravery and

sensitivity are needed. Patience and resilience to disappointment are a given. It is spectacular to watch at top level and uniquely, since novice horses are brought on by the top riders, a place where genuine hobby competitors can find themselves in the same section as Olympic medallists at events.

In 1977 the movie director, Bryan Forbes, had the inspired idea of doing a sequel to the Elizabeth Taylor *Grand National* epic. In the original La Taylor was a schoolgirl who dreamed of winning the Grand National. In great Hollywood tradition the course went clockwise in some US set, whereas Aintree goes the other way...same problem with the Royal Ascot scenes in *My Fair Lady*, by the way!

Forbes' story was of the Taylor 'niece', played by Tatum O'Neil, who aspired to ride at the Olympics. It was largely shot at Burghley in the couple of weeks after the European Championships. About a dozen riders that included Richard Meade, Jane Holderness-Roddam and Ginny Holgate, were deputised as stunt riders. Jane was doubling for Tatum, who was effectively playing the Jane role when she won team gold for Britain at the Mexico Olympics.

The Acting Union rules at the time meant that the doubles had stunt doubles too, so there were all sorts of identical people wandering about the set. There were mornings where the guest riders would go out and somewhat nonchalantly play 'chase me Charlie' over what had been the European course of the previous week.

The film often gets repeated at Christmas in the UK, and is a happy memory, no doubt for the riders who spent a few weeks of that summer working for MGM. It was another useful bit of PR for a sport which, for understandable reasons, was a bit hard to follow.

The 'posh people falling into ponds' image has sometimes been hard to throw off, but over time the dedication and genuine bravery of the contestants have attracted a keen and dedicated following.

The Major Events

As mentioned in the history section, Eventing was a variable sport which had been at the Olympics since 1912, but underwent very many changes until it found itself a fairly consistent formula. The rules change on an almost yearly basis, but only rarely have major changes altered the sport significantly.

Below is a selection of many of the events that sprang up as the sport became more popular. Some have fallen by the wayside, some reappear for a specific championships and some (Olympics) are strictly one-offs.

As noted, until after the war Eventing was a military test which only had a genuinely public outing at the Olympic Games. (There had been some regional military contests, such as the Nordic Games, which continued spasmodically with minimal competitors until 1986.) The first Badminton changed all this and slowly a network in Britain, then a season of events, spawned similar non-Olympic competitions abroad.

The proliferation of Three Day Events, the ultimate point of the sport, spread. Badminton showed that this type of contest was of interest to all-round riders of backgrounds which were equestrian, but with no particular military background. The administration, however, remained the province of the retired officer until the middle 1980s.

With increasing interest in the sport, Badminton was asked to host the first

Above:
Gatcombe

European Championships in 1953. There were 40 riders from six nations, and three teams. Most of the competitors were from the host nation, which duly won. Switzerland took up the organising challenge and ran the second one at Basle the following year. There were now five teams in a smaller field of 27, and Britain won again, but a groundswell of support for spreading the sport was rising.

Playing a bit safe the International Federation awarded the 1955 European Championships to Badminton again, but the twist was that the Queen offered Windsor as 'Badminton', so another venue was christened. Britain again easily fielded the largest number of riders, and won the spoils for the third time. A bye year ensued in 1952 for the Helsinki Games and the Scandinavian axis, with their long history of cavalry contests, put on the Europeans again in 1957.

Badminton became the benchmark for all Three Day Events and is acknowledged as the individual, unofficial world championships.

Badminton has long since outgrown its original purpose as an Olympic testing ground. Indeed, since the Olympic movement has insisted on wider participation, and therefore a median level of test, Badminton and its other highest rated brothers, like Burghley, are significantly more of a challenge.

Badminton is now established as the world's premier event and is the one which the occasional Olympic, World, European or regional Champion, who has never even ridden there before, has to put on their 'bucket list', to ever be considered as a 'real' Eventer.

The success of the first Badminton suggested the possibility of an autumn fixture and in 1953 Harewood Horse Trials began. It again was a bit of an article of faith that anyone would want to enter, and in its first years only managed about 20 entries. Harewood was, however, awarded the 1959 European Championships which attracted 63 entries from 11 countries. Gold medallist was the 1951 Badminton winner, Hans Schwarzenbach, this time on Burn Trout, with Frank Weldon second riding Samuel Johnson.

This turned out to be Harewood's

swansong and 1960 had no big autumn Eventing fixture in the UK, while attention was fixed on the Rome Olympics.

The demise of Harewood spawned the great autumn event which is Burghley. At its first running in 1961, it was won by the outright star combination of the era, Anneli Drummond-Hay and Merely-a-Monarch, by just short of 34 penalties. (Scoring has evolved, but that was still a massive margin).

The first Burghley, however, only had 19 runners and nine finishers. It is easy to forget how tentative the beginnings of the major events were.

The sport was still relatively new and a proven, (by one year), organisation was awarded the 6th European Championships. To current readers the fact that the Soviet Union not only entered a team, but won team gold and individual silver seems unimaginable, but they did. There were 27 starters for that and then the number still hovered at about 30 until 1966.

There have been Asian Games, Pan American Games and even Alpine Games over the years, but usually with few competitors and little significance, apart

from introducing the sport to slightly unnatural terrain. Any riders from these outposts have had to head either for Europe, Australasia or North America to get any type of match practice.

With Badminton as the main spring event, which had, in the sport's infancy, hosted the two European Championships, it became the norm to run medal contests during the autumn season. Whereas Badminton enjoyed its reputation as the unofficial individual world championships, and soon discarded any thought of team competitions, Burghley was perfectly placed to host

these competitions.

1966 saw the first ever World Eventing Championships at Burghley and had 39 entries from five countries. Still, only just over half completed, but that was quite acceptable then. The winner was Capt. Carlos Moratorio from Argentina with Chalan. In twelfth place was Alison Oliver, who would go on to train Princess Anne to European gold. William Fox-Pitt's mother, Marietta Speed, was also in the field that year.

The Burghley estate is the seat of the Cecil family, and Burghley House is one of the best examples of Elizabethan

architecture. The park, much more undulating than Badminton, was landscaped by Capability Brown in the eighteenth century, but the house, predating the park by two hundred years, is reputed to have been designed to resemble a town. There are towers and steeples and roofs at different heights. The coaching town of Stamford is adjacent to the estate.

The first host of the Burghley Horse Trials was the Marquess of Exeter, celebrated as the 'Chariots of Fire' Olympic hurdling gold medallist. His daughter, Lady Victoria Leatham, an antiques expert on the BBC show *The Antiques Road Show*, then ran the house until handing over to her daughter.

Where Badminton relied on former riders and keen foxhunters to design the courses, Burghley Cross Country, from the start, was the inspiration of equestrian vet, Bill Thompson, (who moonlighted as a Cross Country commentator at Badminton).

Bill's courses tended to have very widespread fences, which looked formidable when walked, but actually jumped without too much of a problem, even surprisingly from a trot, if needed.

Bill found natural features, such as the Trout Hatchery, Capability's Cutting, the Dairy Mound and The Leaf Pit, to place his obstacles, which have since become Burghley standards.

After Bill, the designing task went to the man responsible for making the turf at Burghley the most renowned on the international circuit, the Clerk of the Course, Philip Herbert. He has retained that role since Mark Phillips took over the designing job.

Mark's riding history, as with both Frank Weldon and Hugh Thomas at Badminton, lent him a different authority over the course and certainly Mark's courses have raised the bar at Burghley to an extent that there is not much to choose between the difficulty of Badminton and its autumn relation.

When Mark had to take a Sabbatical when Burghley hosted an 'Open European Championships', to train his USA riders, the job went to Badminton and Burghley runner-up and TV commentator, Mike Tucker, who had for many years run an event at his Tetbury farm.

Burghley hit the news when Princess Anne and Doublet became the tenth European Champions in 1971 and the Lincolnshire venue then hosted the 1974 World Championships, which recorded the high point of USA Eventing, with Bruce Davidson taking gold and Mike Plumb, silver. They also took the team gold with their colleagues, Don Sachey and Edward Emmerson.

Badminton's early timing in the year may still make it the tougher challenge, but any rider completing Burghley will have earned their 'grown up' Eventing spurs.

It was apt, considering the military history of the sport, that the army garrison town of Tidworth would become the host to the third British Three Day Event. In the late Sixties and early Seventies there was a clear 'career path' for aspiring Eventers, both equine and human. Tidworth ran several sections, based on points scored at earlier competitions, but rather like the old days of Little and Great Badminton, the Cross Country was the same for all.

If you had enjoyed a good Tidworth in the May, you would chance a go at Burghley that September, and if that went fine you would dare to take on Badminton the following spring.

Indeed, for several years Tidworth held the selection Trial for the British

Junior team.

Tidworth was a bit of a production line Three Day Event with several Dressage arenas operating at the same time on the garrison polo field, which also ran simultaneous horse trot ups, and all this done to a stage set castle wall, left over from the previous week's military tattoo. The going on the Roads and Tracks was rough and in some places quite flinty.

Because there were quite a lot of competitors at Tidworth, all doing the same course and on site for the week, with established and Junior riders (whose Cross Country was the day before the seniors) there was a very sociable atmosphere. In the days before large, smart horse boxes where the competitors now live, riders would line the polo field at the competitors' caravan park and on the night after the Cross Country there was a ball into the small hours at the Officers' Mess at Tedworth House.

The Duke of Bedford's younger brother, Lord Hugh Russell, had been an enthusiastic amateur Eventer, and his wife 'Lady Hugh' had ridden at top level until she was confined to a wheelchair after a hunting fall. Their farm in Wiltshire became the training base for the British team, and Lady Hugh, despite her incapacity, became one of the world's most respected, indeed feared, Cross Country trainers. She would bark instructions to the very best, like Richard Meade and Lucinda Prior-Palmer, with a megaphone from her distinctive Mini Moke.

The Russells' remarkably hilly property at Wylye was littered with all types of Cross Country obstacles, which, when not used for training, made an ideal setting for multi-class competitions. It may not have looked pretty, but Wylye became the perfect place to run a Tidworth level autumn Three Day Event. The farm was dissected by a new motorway, but the event, which started modestly as a One Day Event, became a Three Day Event and eventually became a fully fledged International affair. Lady Hugh took up competitive carriage driving quite late in life, despite her disability, and Wylye hosted a carriage driving competition alongside the ridden event.

The horse trial made good use of all the myriad practice jumps, so that a Wylye completion put a horse in good stead for moving up the Three Day Event ladder.

There were of course events on the Continent, which were attracting the more adventurous competitors. With Burghley seemingly hosting an international Championships about every three years, Boekelo in Holland became the refuge of those not selected for Burghley. It is now one of the most popular autumn competitions on the European Circuit.

Punchestown in Ireland had hosted European and World Championships and was a firm fixture for travelling British riders. In the long format days horses would only aim for one Three Day Event in the spring and another in the autumn, and even the top riders at the time probably only had a couple of horses to ride, so with the lower level Tidworths and Wylyes as stepping stones to the Badmintons and Burghleys, most British riders only ventured abroad if they were selected for a Championships,

or found a run at somewhere like Boekelo if the autumn championships were being held, as they quite regularly were at Burghley.

There were raiding parties to Germany and France, Belgium and Holland, but the world of the major Three Day Event remained English.

Bramham Park in Yorkshire was the next place to host a Three Day Event in Britain and became the venue for the Young Rider selection system for the GB squad. More importantly, it became the place where both Mary King and Ian Stark presented their credentials to the Eventing world.

Bramham, unlike Tidworth and Wylye and the racecourse or golf course venues at other internationals, hosted its event in the perfect British setting of a really stately park. Riders on the Endurance sections would have the similar privilege of riding up beautiful avenues as they would at places like Badminton and Burghley.

Yorkshire has a great tradition in following horse sports and Bramham has also run high grade Show Jumping as part of the attraction to its event.

Bramham has also been the testing ground for both Sue Benson, who

designed Greenwich, and Ian Stark, as course builders of international repute.

As mentioned, in 1955 Badminton took a year at Windsor at the invitation of the Queen. In the Seventies an event started in the Great Park based round the Polo pitches at Smith's Lawn. Under the direction of Peggy Maxwell this then became a Two Day Event. The Two Day Event was something of a Mrs. Maxwell

invention, as she had spawned one at Tweseldown Racecourse, Crookham, scene of the 1948 Olympic 'chase phase of the Eventing Endurance section. The Two Day Event started with Dressage and then Show Jumping but the next day the Cross Country would be preceded by Roads and Tracks and a Steeplechase phase. It was like a mini dry run for the Badmintons and Burghleys. As a concept

Left: *Tidworth*

they never really took off. Osberton and Chepstow, Wing and LLanfechain ran them for a few years, but with Princess Anne's help, Windsor matured into a real Three Day Event in 1979. It then moved to a different part of the park, straddling the Long Walk, with Windsor Castle as a backdrop. In its early days the event had the honour of the Queen being there on Show Jumping day and presenting the prizes. At Windsor these were rather grand, having been appropriated from some long gone polo tournaments.

The only trouble with Windsor was that the clay soil could either bake hard and rutty, or be very deep. Also in the early years stabling had to be at Ascot Racecourse. The courses had the best designers, however, since Burghley's Bill Thompson and future Badminton

Right: *Bramham*

designer, Hugh Thomas, made their mark on the Park.

Rotherfield Park in Hampshire became a Three Day Event venue, which hosted back to back Junior and Young Rider Championships, and was Hugh Thomas's calling card as a designer. As a very young man Hugh had designed a very testing Pony Club Eventing course at his Hampshire home near Alton.

The house at Rotherfield Park was used for exterior shots for a TV adaptation of the Daphne du Maurier book, *Rebecca*.

In the early days only Badminton and Burghley, as Three Day Events, mustered any type of crowd, but in the perfect setting of Chatsworth in Derbyshire, the annual One Day Event was an equally important outing. For a short time in the 1980s Chatsworth joined the ranks of Three Day Event, but returned to One Day status, albeit at International level.

Now that organisers no longer have to provide miles of Roads and Tracks and a Steeplechase course, it is much easier to put on a Three Day Event, one of the reasons for the change, to help emerging countries, but apart from distances and speeds, there is not much to differentiate between the ultimate level of the sport

and the run-up level.

There are British Three Day Events at Weston Park and Hartpury and a popular one north of the border at Blair Castle in Scotland.

There is now a considerable International circuit. France runs a top level Three Day Event at the end of the year at Pau near the Pyrenees and Le Lion D'Anger hosts the younger horse championships. These French events have a very stylish Gallic air, very different to the Stately Home British

venues. As at many foreign competitions they are both held around racing set ups on sandy tracks and pine woods. They have a rather more casual feel to the British events.

As mentioned, Holland runs a very popular trials at Boekelo on an unsurprisingly flat course that surrounds a riding centre, and Germany has a purpose built equestrian centre at Aachen which hosts Championship classes in all three Olympic disciplines of Dressage, Jumping and Eventing. It was here that

Zara Phillips added the world title to her European one. Germany has hosted a Three Day Event at Achshelswang and a top level one at Luhmhulen.

The main event in the USA is at Lexington, known generically by its sponsor's name just as 'Rolex'. The first time a Three Day Event was held there was for the 1978 World Championships.

Australia has run events at Gawler and Adelaide, where the antipodean riders can stake their team credentials against their compatriots who have based themselves in Europe. One of Australia's top riders, Philip Dutton, based himself in the USA and eventually took citizenship there.

The sport has had National championships for many years, being hosted at Wylye, Cirencester Park, Locko Park in Derbyshire, and for many years at Princess Anne's Park at Gatcombe. In the old days there was a Novice Championships and an Open Championships, and they were sufficiently important to have been televised. Next, an Intermediate class was added and Gatcombe is now rebranded as The Festival of British Eventing.

The whole history of Eventing completed an elegant circle in 2012. It was the Aldershot Olympics in 1948 that got the ball rolling and with the Games coming to London, Greenwich was chosen as the strictly one-off venue for all the equestrian competitions.

This was not without controversy as the obvious short term use of the park, led to accusations that there would be no lasting legacy. In truth, no Olympic Eventing venue has survived, so Greenwich would not be alone. What Greenwich did offer, however, was an historic, very British location, that was right amongst the rest of the Games, with a total London skyline as its backdrop.

Planning requirements were incredibly onerous to comply with, but after all the work and smiling gods, it turned out to be arguably the venue of the entire games. Sue Benson's course had, as all Olympic tracks do, to make it achievable for the emerging equestrian nations, but create a proper result among the experienced squads. Her jumps looked on the gentle side when viewed individually, but the steep slopes and tight turns all played their part and an excellent competition ensued, followed, of course, by a triumph in the other equestrian disciplines on the specially constructed raised arena.

Personalities of the Sport

Pre-war Eventing was an entirely military affair, but it was strictly for the officer class only. At the Berlin Olympics in 1936 the home side expediently promoted their best rider from the Other Ranks to Captain. Thus Capt. Ludwig Stubbendorff won both individual and team gold on Nurmi.

The sport only became known outside military circles with the organisation of the first ever Badminton. Almost by definition Badminton's first winner became its first star. Like many of the early event riders in the late 1940s, John Shedden had served in the army, but he had since become a professional riding instructor. This barred him as a contender for Olympic selection, as the Games were still for amateurs only. As a professional, he was one of the few early British Eventers who had got the hang of Dressage. A decent test in that phase and a storming Cross Country round on the strong pulling American thoroughbred, Golden Willow, gave him an unassailable lead on the final day.

The following year he entered both Golden Willow, on which he came fifth and Kingpin who was runner-up. It was, however, Golden Willow's incredible leap, jumping the high and wide Irish Bank in one bound, which made the headlines.

That second Badminton was won by another ex-army professional horseman. Capt. Tony Collings did easily the best

Dressage tests at the first two Badmintons on Remus, and, like Shedden, he was ineligible for British team inclusion. He instead became team trainer up to the 1952 Games, and also senior instructor at what was to become the home of British equestrianism for some years, Porlock Vale Riding School in Somerset.

Major Frank Weldon had always had an ambition to ride in the Grand National, though he was thwarted by qualification. He had spent much of a frustrating war as a prisoner in Germany, and by 1952 he was commanding the King's Troop RHA and had been preoccupied with the problem of extending the equestrian pursuits of his keen young officers, who were used mainly to hunting and racing. The C/O and four other officers entered Badminton that year, though with no great success. Weldon himself had a crashing fall from Liza Mandy at a hazelwood jump with a drop. The following year, which was the first European Championships, he rode the impressive Kilbarry into second place and a team gold. The pair were also runners-up in 1954.

The next European Championships were held at Windsor in 1955 (though officially a 'Badminton' by Royal appointment). Weldon and Kilbarry did one better and won both team and individual gold. They were very much the top combination of their era, winning Harewood in the autumn of that year, and they consolidated this by winning Badminton proper in 1956.

Weldon's greatest legacy to the sport, however, was as course designer and director of Badminton. He introduced some of the trademark 'rider frightener' fences such as the Normandy Bank and Ski Jump.

Vivien Machin-Goodall was the first lady to complete the inaugural Badminton, coming fifth with Neptune, blazing the trail for future female stars. She was the first lady to win an international Three Day Event on the same horse at Harewood in 1953. Margaret Hough was the first to win Badminton on Bambi V in 1954, but it was the striking blonde, Sheila Willcox, who staked her claim to fame, by coming runner-up to Weldon and Kilbarry in 1956 riding High and Mighty. What might have developed into an exciting rivalry was undone by Kilbarry suffering a fatal fall at the first fence of a warm-up contest at Cottesbrooke the following year.

Willcox and High and Mighty won

Far Left: *Frank Weldon*

PERSONALITIES OF THE SPORT

Badminton 1957 to an extent unopposed, going last and leading in all phases. They went on to become European Champions at Copenhagen that year. They, like Weldon and Kilbarry before them, were unstoppable and took the Badminton title again in 1958. In 1959, now as Mrs. Waddington, Sheila made it a hat-trick, by winning Badminton with Airs and Graces.

Lana Dupont of the USA made history by becoming the first lady rider to take part in an Olympic Games earning a team silver with Mr. Wister at Tokyo in 1964.

Australian farmer, Bill Roycroft, has two claims to fame. He was part of the Australian Olympic squad that came to Britain by slow boat en route to the Rome Games of 1960. He won Badminton that year with Our Solo and helped Australia win team gold in the summer. He did the latter drugged up after discharging himself from hospital following a heavy fall on the Cross Country, which had concussed him. In 1965 he became the first of only two people to ride three horses round Badminton in a day, with Eldorado, Stoney Crossing and Avatar. The other was Scotland's Lorna Sutherland who

repeated the feat in 1970 with Popadom, Gypsy Flame and The Dark Horse.

Lorna had a long and distinguished Eventing career. She won Burghley in 1967 with her hogged (clipped maned) skewbald (brown and white) 'circus' horse, Popadum, and was third there again in 1969, also coming ninth with Gypsy Flame, another coloured horse. In 1978 she won Burghley another time, as Mrs. Clarke, on this occasion with Greco. She was second there with Danville in 1984 and won team gold and individual silver the next year with Myross at the Europeans. In 1986 the pair were team gold and individual bronze at the World Championships. Lorna first rode at Badminton in 1967, coming eighth with Nicholas Nickelby, and finally retired from riding there in 1992 after a then record of 22 completions of the great event. On her competitive retirement Lorna commentated on the sport for the BBC for several years.

By the 1960s Great Britain was by far the world centre of Eventing, so although previous Olympic team and individual medallists were no doubt feted in their own countries for their wins, the sport at which they had triumphed was less heralded. In 1968,

LITTLE BOOK OF **EVENTING**

however, Badminton had been won by student nurse, Jane Bullen, on her diminutive Our Nobby from Richard Meade on Turnstone and Staff Sergeant Ben Jones and Foxdor. Major Derek Allhusen was fifth with Lochinvar. These four were to be the British team at the Mexico Olympics. In those days even top riders were expected to lend their horses for the national good, and Martin Whiteley, an Eton schoolmaster, who had won Little Badminton in 1965 with The Poacher, was fifth at the first World Championships in 1966 at Burghley and had won individual silver at the 1967 Europeans at Punchestown, Ireland. Martin made the horse available for Ben Jones. Richard Meade took the ride on the incapacitated Mary Gordon-Watson's Cornishman V.

In heroic circumstances, after a waterlogged Cross Country day, the British prevailed and Allhusen took individual silver. The golden galloping nurse made the headlines, and Meade put himself in the position of being almost able to command any ride he wanted. Mary Gordon-Watson had the satisfaction of becoming European Champion with Cornishman V the following year at Haras du Pin, in France, third at Badminton 1970 and then World Champion that autumn at Punchestown.

The 1967 silver medallist at the first Junior Europeans, which only fielded 10 riders from Britain and France, was South African born, British rider, Richard Walker with Pasha. The following year, when 46 riders from eight countries made it a real contest, Walker and Pasha took gold. Fresh from that they came to Badminton in 1969, where Richard remains the youngest ever winner, aged 18. They went on to take senior individual silver and team gold at the Europeans in France that year. After some years away from top flight competition, Richard returned to win Burghley in 1980 with John of Gaunt, and again with Ryan's Cross in 1982.

By 1970 Richard Meade had the ride on The Poacher and won Badminton 1970 on him. The pair were silver medallist to Mary Gordon-Watson at the World Championships. Mary and Cornishman came second at Badminton in 1971 to Mark Phillips and Great Ovation.

That year the sport got a massive publicity boost when Princess Anne

Far Left: *Lorna Sutherland*

came fifth on her Badminton debut and followed that up by becoming European Champion with Doublet on home ground at Burghley in September.

Mark, after his impressive fourth placed Badminton debut in 1968 with Rock On, had missed out on the Mexico Olympics, but they came seventh as individuals at the 1969 European Championships at Haras du Pin. Mark, still a serving officer, was by now basing his riding activities at the West Country yard of former Olympic rider, Bertie Hill. Bertie had been well placed at Badminton 1970 with Chicago III but they were disqualified for taking the wrong course in the Jumping phase. Phillips took the ride on Chicago at the second World Championships at Punchestown and was part of the gold medal team with Mary Gordon-Watson and Richard Meade, alongside another Bertie protégé, Stuart Stevens and Benson. By Burghley 1971, he and his Badminton winner, Great Ovation, were part of the European gold winning team.

In 1972 Mark and Great Ovation won Badminton for the second time, to put them into contention for the Munich Olympics, as did Richard

Meade, now astride the Allhusen-bred Laureston, who came second. Third at Badminton that year was West Country 'Bertie' rider, Bridget Parker, with Cornish Gold. These three were joined at Munich by the reliable, proven pair of Mary Gordon-Watson and Cornishman. The team triumphed and Richard Meade, who had been previously linked to Princess Anne, won individual gold.

In Britain the sport was, by now, not only well known because of the Royal connections, but because its riders had won team Olympics back to back. It now also had an individual Olympic Champion.

At Burghley Mark Phillips again got the ride on another horse from the Hill yard. This time it was the mare, Maid Marion, who had previously been ridden by Bertie's son, Tony, to individual silver and team gold at the 1972 Junior Europeans at Eridge. She wasn't an easy ride, but not for the first time Phillips managed to conjure up a great performance on a chance ride and win the event.

Phillips went on to win three Badmintons in four years, the first two with his aunt Flavia's Great Ovation, and in 1974 on the Queen's Columbus, which had become too much of a handful for Princess Anne. In the meantime he and Princess Anne had got married, further propelling the sport into the limelight.

All eyes were on Mark and Columbus at the 1974 World Championships at Burghley, but sadly they pulled up lame after the Cross Country, having put themselves into a winning position. He had several other rides at top level and won Badminton in 1981 with Lincoln, just ahead of Sandy Pflueger and Free Scott. Sandy would later become the second Mrs. Phillips.

Mark went on to train the US

Eventing team for over 20 years and became one of the world's leading course designers, starting the British Open at his former home, Gatcombe Park, and also at Burghley.

The interim winner of Badminton, in 1973, was Lucinda Prior-Palmer, a granddaughter of a Viceroy of India, who was to embark on a staggering run of wins at the world's toughest event. Emerging from the Royal Artillery Pony Club on Salisbury Plain, Lucinda and Be Fair were part of the gold medal British team at the Junior European Championships in 1971 at Wesel, Germany, coming a respectable, but by no means special eleventh individually. A hint of the success to follow was revealed when the pair came fifth at their next big outing, their first attempt at Badminton in 1972. Missing out on selection for the 1972 Munich Olympics, their Badminton win made them first choice for inclusion for their first senior team selection for the European Championships at Kiev, in what was then the Soviet Union. 20 of the 43 starters failed to complete the basically dangerous Cross Country course (watched by unsuspecting local 'rent-a-crowd'). The British team picked up a brave bronze thanks to

Janet Hodgson remounting Larkspur after a crashing fall at the notorious second fence, a downhill parallel over a ditch. Lucinda and Be Fair were twelfth individually. Badminton 1974 was something of a disaster for Lucinda and Be Fair. They had an early stop at The Quarry and then a fall at a new S fence. They still went as individuals to the Burghley World Championships that year and came tenth. Badminton 1975 was cancelled, but Lucinda and Be Fair became European Champions that year at Luhmuhlen, Germany.

On Badminton's return in 1976 Lucinda rode Wideawake, a horse she had taken a bit of time to gel with. They duly won the event, but tragedy was to strike after the prize giving, when Wideawake reared up and dropped down dead.

George had been ridden by Matt Straker at the Junior Europeans in 1972 and had completed Badminton with him in 1973 and 1974. Military duties for Matt in 1976 provided a chance ride for Canadian, Robert Desourdy, who completed with the horse in 1976. George had, however, fallen on five previous outings when Lucinda, somewhat gingerly, took the ride for

Far Left: *Mark Phillips*

Badminton 1977. The pair won by over 20 penalties and went on to become European Champions that year at Burghley, picking up a team gold into the bargain. Lucinda was third at Badminton that year with Killaire and second the next year with Village Gossip.

Killaire, something of a one paced galloper, had his moment in the sun when Lucinda won Badminton 1979

on him and they were runners-up the following year to the unknown Mark Todd with Southern Comfort.

The Moscow Games of 1980 were boycotted by several Western countries, and even Sports Federations within those countries who decided to go, elected not to send teams. Though Sebastian Coe achieved golden glory as a runner in Moscow to little opprobrium, the riders, vociferously, especially in Lucinda's case, decided to make a political stand. The enormous irony is that this rather naive stance was taken as a protest to the USSR invasion of Afghanistan. London 2012 received no such boycott!

The 'refusnik' equestrian competition took place at Fontainebleau, France, later in the year, which even included some riders who had ridden in Moscow. For what it is worth, Lucinda and Village Gossip came seventh individually, and the British team failed to complete.

Lucinda won Burghley 1981 with Beagle Bay, and then in 1982, by this time married to Australian rider, David Green, Lucinda was seventh and eighth at Badminton with Regal Realm and Beagle Bay. David pipped her by coming sixth with Mairangi Bay.

Lucinda and Regal Realm became world Champions that year at Luhmuhlen.

In 1983 Lucinda won her fifth Badminton with Regal Realm, and individual silver at that year's Europeans at Frauenfeld, Switzerland. The following year Lucinda broke her own outstanding record by winning her sixth Badminton with Beagle Bay.

It was only the Olympic Games

where Lucinda never quite shone to the extent that her other achievements might have predicted. Since retiring from top level competing, Lucinda has been an inspirational Cross Country trainer and a commentator for TV. Her enormous experience has also been put to use as a British team selector.

Ginny Holgate was Junior European Champion in 1973 with Dubonnet and won the Olympic test event at Montreal in 1975 on her second string, Jason. A promising senior career was cut short by a serious fall, where Ginny broke her arm so badly that amputation was seriously considered. Fortunately it did mend, but Ginny's comeback was marred to start with by bad luck and mistakes.

It wasn't until the maturity of Priceless and Night Cap II that she entered a purple patch, reflected coincidently by her purple Cross Country colours. In 1980 Priceless was sixth at Burghley and eighth at Badminton in 1981; at Burghley 1981 Night Cap was third. Badminton 1982 saw Priceless fourth and in the gold medal team at the Worlds that year, with Night Cap fifth at Burghley.

Night Cap was eleventh at Badminton 1983 and Priceless won Burghley that year. Priceless won individual bronze and

team silver at the Los Angeles Olympics in 1984 and Night Cap won Burghley. Ginny went on to win Badminton in 1985 with Priceless, where Night Cap was third. At Burghley 1985 it was Europeans again, when Priceless won individual and team gold.

Night Cap was fourth at Badminton in 1986, and Ginny, now Mrs. Leng, triumphed with Priceless for team and individual gold at the Worlds at Gawler, Australia. She'd taken gold in a secondary 'world championships', for those unable to travel to Australia that autumn, with Night Cap, and just to ring the changes, won Burghley that year on the very strong pulling Murphy Himself. Ian Stark subsequently took the ride after Ginny had a heavy fall from the grey at the next Badminton to run in 1988. However the return of Badminton, after the cancellation of 1987, saw the emergence of a new stable star for Ginny, who was by now living at Acton Turville in hacking distance from Badminton Park.

Master Craftsman came third there, and went on to win in 1989. Master Craftsman was second at Badminton in 1992 where Ginny had a heavy fall from Welton Houdini. To freshen him up

Above: *Bill Roycroft*

she took him hunting that season, and he came back to win Badminton 1993. Ginny had also met her second husband, Mikey Elliot, in the hunting field. At her height Ginny became the TV face of Oil of Ulay.

Pippa Nolan was another of the relatively few to emerge into the senior ranks after success at Junior and Young Rider level. Pippa first rode for Britain as member of the bronze team in Germany in 1986 with Airborne III. She then won gold in the younger divisions with Sir Barnaby on whom she made her Badminton debut in 1988.

It was with Supreme Rock and Primmore's Pride that Pippa was to make her name, which by then was

Mrs. Funnell! She became European Champion twice in a row with Rocky in 1999 and 2001. She won her first Badminton on the same horse in 2002. In 2003 Pippa took the first prize at Rolex, Lexington, by a whisker of a technical score difference to the runner-up on the same penalty with Primmore's Pride. Pippa then came straight to Badminton to win again with Supreme Rock the following week. This time by just point four of a penalty. This set Funnell up for a chance of the Rolex Grand Slam, for winning Rolex Badminton and Burghley on the trot (in any order).

Primmore's Pride duly won Burghley and Pippa became the first to take the $250,000 prize. As is the character building nature of the sport, at the following Badminton Pippa fell from both her rides at the same fence.

She bounced back from that, however, to win Badminton 2005 with Primmore's Pride.

Mary Thomson came from a completely 'unhorsey' family, but was fascinated by the vicar's pony, which she persuaded her mother to lead round the Salcombe Regis lanes. She rode all sorts including a donkey, but it was a visit to Badminton at the age of 11, with her local Axe Vale Pony Club, that she became determined that Eventing was to be her sport.

Mary subsidised her early riding by doing all sorts of odd jobs to finance her dream. She then became a pupil at early Badminton multiple winner Sheila Willcox's establishment, where she learnt the benefits of utter dedication and commitment.

Mary also travelled and crewed on the tall ship, Winston Churchill, before setting up on her own. Her first stables were a couple of converted cow sheds, and Mary kept the operation going, selling horses, working as a domestic, gardening and delivering meat.

In 1985 she came seventh at Badminton on Diver's Rock and for once turned down good money to continue her bid for equestrian stardom. This paid off as she soon secured sponsorship. The following year, at the step up Three Day Event at Bramham, she came first and second on King Cuthbert and Silverstone and then came second at Badminton in 1989 with King Boris, and eighth with Cuthbert. At Burghley that year the positions were reversed, with Cuthbert in second and Boris fourth.

In 1991 Mary won a European team

gold with King William, (most of Mary's rides are prefixed with King, and indeed she married cattle farmer, David King.) Her first major win was at Badminton 1992 with King William.

In 1995 Mary and King William won team gold and individual bronze at the World Championships in Italy and Mary won Burghley in 1996 with Star Appeal. She went on to win the premier event at Badminton again in 2000 with that horse. The following year she broke her neck in a fall at home, but she was back at the top a year later, coming third at Burghley with King Solomon.

All in all Mary has won six team gold medals at World and European Championships and has been British Champion four times. She rode in six consecutive Olympic Games, starting at Barcelona in 1992, achieving team bronze in 2008 with Call Again Cavalier and team silver at Greenwich in 2012 with Imperial Cavalier.

Along with Pippa Funnell, Mary has a very keen fan base amongst aspiring young girls.

New Zealander, Sir Mark Todd, is the only equestrian to be knighted for his services to the sport. He competed without any inkling of what was to come at the World Championships at Lexington in 1978, getting eliminated on the Cross Country with Top Hunter. He then came over to Britain to ride Southern Comfort at Badminton in 1980. In a challenging year, and surviving a slip up at the notorious Foot Bridge fence, they emerged surprise winners.

It wasn't until 1984, when he came second at Badminton with Charisma IV, that Todd's potential was about to be fulfilled. That year they went on to win individual gold at the Los Angeles Olympics and returned to second spot at Badminton the following year. Mark and Charisma went on to take individual gold at the Seoul Olympics in 1988.

Mark developed a reputation as a 'super sub'. In 1989 he took over the Badminton ride of the injured Rodney Powell on The Irishman, (Rodney won on him two years later). In 1994, this time taking the reins from the injured Lynne Bevan on Horton Point, riding with the number one they won the event, which Todd did again two years on with the former Nick Burton ride, Bertie Blunt.

Mark was equally successful at Burghley. He won it first in 1987 with Wilton Fair and back to back in 1990

Left: *Sir Mark Todd*

Right: *Ginny Holgate*

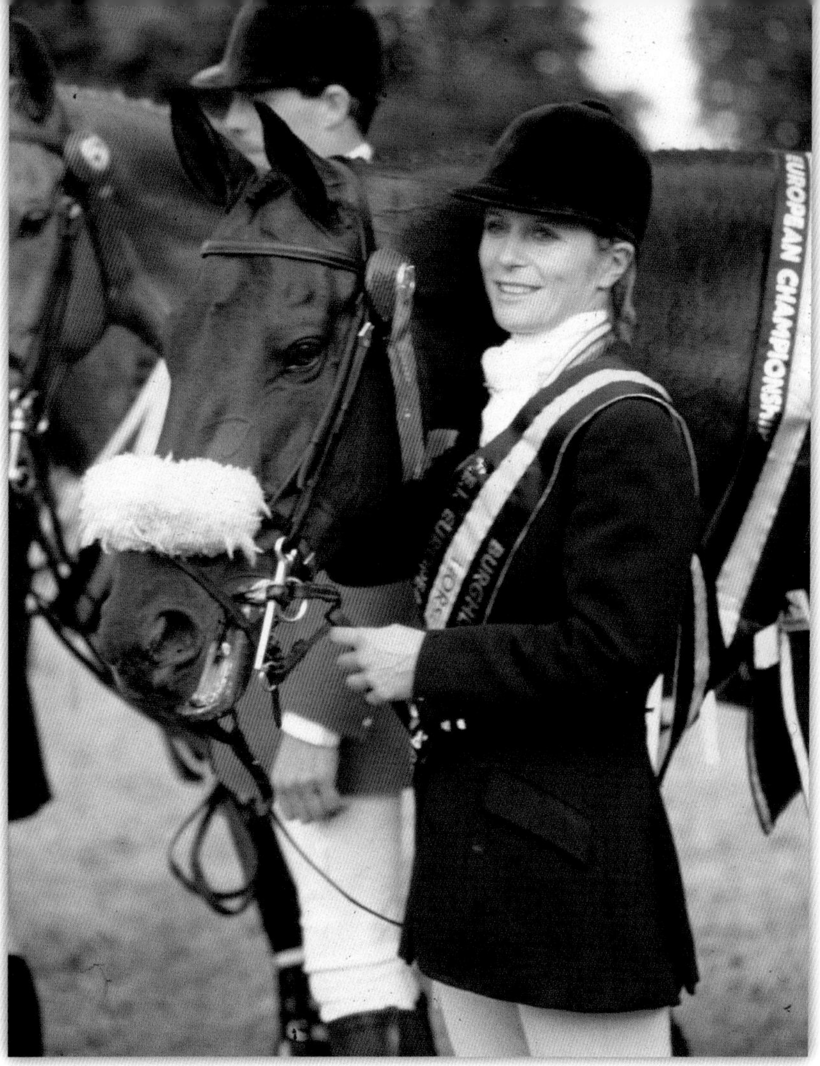

and 1991, with Face the Music and Welton Greylag. In 1997 Burghley ran as an Open European Championships, as a one-off, and Mark won gold riding Broadcast News. He most recently won Burghley in 1999 on Diamond Hall Red, before announcing his retirement from the sport at top level after the Sydney Olympics. He subsequently returned to New Zealand and successfully trained racehorses, taking the Wellington Cup and the New Zealand Oaks. He also coached the NZ team for the Athens Olympics, after which the seed of an idea was planted.

Almost as a joke challenge, Mark decided to start a campaign to ride at Beijing and bought the 10-year-old Gandalf and secured sponsorship with New Zealand Bloodstock. After a relatively successful return Olympic appearance, Mark made a full return to elite level Eventing and came back to base himself, once more, in England.

His return was completed when he won Badminton 2011 with NZB Land Vision. Mark was given the accolade of 'Rider of the Twentieth Century' by the FEI (International Equestrian Federation) and is staking his claim to the twenty-first century title too.

Andrew Nicholson came over from New Zealand to work as groom to Mark Todd. He very soon established himself as an international competitor in his own right. Like Todd he has been to six Olympic Games, though with mixed fortunes. He achieved a disappointing team silver at the Barcelona Olympics, when his ride, Spinning Rhombus, knocked down nine show jumps to hand gold to arch rivals, Australia. He won a happier team bronze at Atlanta with Jagermeister II.

Nicholson has a good Burghley record, winning for the first time in 1995 with Buckley Province and again in 2000 on Mr. Smiffy. Twelve years on he won again with Avebury.

At Badminton Andrew's best result was second in 2004 on Lord Killinghurst, but he is best renowned as Badminton's most prolific completer with 31 and counting. He also regularly tops seasonal points' leagues.

Perhaps reflecting the potentially close-knit world of the sport, and its rivalries, Andrew's partner, Wiggy, was formerly married to William Fox-Pitt.

William Fox-Pitt was bred for the job. Both his mother, Marietta, and father, Oliver, competed at international level. William was riding by the age of four and Eventing from 15. Unlike the majority of Eventers today, William was university educated having graduated from the University of London after Eton.

Having come up through Junior ranks, William's first big win was at Burghley in 1994 with Chaka. The following year at Badminton they were overnight leaders after the Cross Country, only to fail the final horse inspection. William has been a stalwart of the British team since 1995, helping to win multiple team golds at European Championships and one at the Worlds. He has won three team silvers and one bronze at the Olympics.

Burghley is William's most successful event. He won it again with Highland Lad in 2002, Ballincoola in 2005, and two in a row in 2007 and 2008 with Parkmore Ed and Tamarillo, on whom he won Badminton in 1994. Tamarillo became the thirteenth horse to win both premier events.

William won a record sixth Burghley in 2011 with Parklane Hawk, and has been six-time leading rider in Britain. He is married to Channel 4 Racing presenter, Alice Plunkett.

Since the development of the sport post-war, it has now become the turn of the next generation to make it to the top. There are, in fact, surprisingly few apart from William, though Richard Meade's son, Harry, has ridden at Badminton level. Zara Phillips came up through the Young Rider programme with Toytown, winning individual European silver, and went on to come second at their debut Burghley. In 2005 they emulated the rider's mother, Princess Anne, by becoming senior European Champion, going one better by taking the world title the following year. All this before riding at Badminton.

Several Badminton rides have yet to prove fruitful, but she made the British squad for the London Games, in a year when Badminton was cancelled, and helped the team to a silver medal, helping enormously to whet the media appetite for the equestrian triumphs to follow.

Like her mother, her background will ensure media interest, as does her marriage to former England rugby captain, Mike Tindall, who was described as only the second best sportsman in his house when Zara, like the Princess, won BBC Sports Personality of the Year.

MITSUBISHI

Trainers

As with all sports even those at the top have to go and be trained. From the old cavalry days it was the army training grounds that put the military riders through their paces. In England this was based for many years at Weedon, but it was after the Second World War that civilian training centres came into their own, albeit with former army instructors.

Tony Collings, as a professional, was ineligible to ride for the British team, but was ideal to become British team trainer.

He based himself at Porlock Vale Riding School in Somerset. Before the war Tony was a well known follower of the Devon and Somerset Staghounds and successful Point to Point rider.

On one of his horses, Grey Sky, he won 17 races, even winning two on the same day. He was also big in the showing world. Attending a course with Col. Jack Hance he was so enthused that he was determined to turn the family establishment at Porlock into a professional training establishment.

It was on his return from hostilities in 1945 that the plans began to come to fruition and of course only three years before the 1948 Olympic Three Day Event at Aldershot, which spawned the first Badminton the following year in 1949. A Yorkshire landowner, Chris Leyland, bought Porlockford House and in partnership with Tony Collings turned the house and buildings, together

with an indoor school, into the yard that was to develop.

One of the early instructors there was Major Dick Hern, another early Eventing enthusiast, who, of course, became the Queen's racehorse trainer.

The setup attracted students from all over the world. On the first day of any course riders were taken for a hack to see how they all rode, and were then put up at a local guest house called The Gables. The girl pupils outnumbered the men four to one, which was a norm at many equestrian establishments.

Dressage was still pretty well unheard of and Porlock hosted the first Dressage course in England since before the war, run naturally by a 'continental', Monsieur Harry Asselbergs, a Belgian. Since rationing was still in full swing the main animal feed was from 7lb tins of condemned army biscuits; rather different to the special diets of today's competition elite.

Quite a lot of the horses at Porlock were bought especially as school horses and came from Exeter market.

In 1948 Porlock had an involvement with the Olympic Games, providing horses for the Modern Pentathlon. In this competition a pool of loaned horses are drawn for the competitors and as recently as Greenwich in 2012, it is always a bit hit and miss as to what a proficient runner, swimmer, fencer and shot might draw for the equestrian

Right: *Yogi Breisner*

element.

As with many a yard there were some jolly times and japes, but as always the nightmare scenario would be a fatal accident to a pupil. A rather mature student of Chris Leyland had a crashing fall while jumping. The instructor feared the worst when he approached the inert body and was fixed with a lifeless stare. Fortunately the rider was only winded, but sported a glass eye.

Saturdays were a respite from serious training and Tony Collings would lead a 'chase me Charlie' out onto the moor. This was a precursor of the 'dare' rides at Bertie Hill's in the Seventies. You can only learn so much. Self-preservation gives you the edge when the 'precious' school riding is thrown to the wind.

Jane Crystal was a regular course attendee at Porlock and owned a useful 16hh hunter called Remus. Tony Collings saw potential in the horse and persuaded Jane to put it into training at Porlock for the first ever Badminton (for him to ride). Since no one had any idea what the course at Badminton would be like, various spying missions to Gloucestershire were arranged. It helped that Collings' step-daughter was at school near Badminton!

Many now remember 1949 as the year of the first Badminton, but Collings, along with Harry Llewlyn and Mike Ansell, put on the first Horse of the Year Show that autumn at Harringay. Collings and Remus went on to win Badminton in 1950. It was after this that it was suggested Porlock would be the training base for the 1952 Helsinki Olympic Eventing team, the initial raison d'être for the innovation of the first Badminton. Usual courses continued at Porlock in the build up to the Games.

Seven riders came down for training: John Miller, later to become Crown Equerry, Laurence Rook, Michael Naylor-Leyland, Angus McCance, John Oram, Reg Hindley and Bertie Hill. In a situation similar to today where the British team is trained by a Swede and the Germans by an Englishman, in 1952 a German, Herr Waetjen, came to assist Collings. He had been an instructor at the Spanish Riding School in Vienna.

Sadly, Tony Collings was killed in the Comet crash of 1954. Porlock carried on, but was never again the team base.

Bertie Hill, who had been to Porlock and was one of the civilian stars of the sport, ran a farm and yard at Great Rapscott, also in the West Country. If

Taylor, who won Badminton in 1967 on Jonathan, Lorna Sutherland who rode three horses round in a day, and Debbie West, all went to Eddy Goldman.

Jane Bullen and Mark Phillips had the good fortune to be in the Beaufort Pony Club and were taught there by Frank Weldon.

By going to an establishment, however, that had half a dozen horses heading for the biggest events, a great team spirit built up at the competition yards and also some healthy rivalry. Younger riders, who were hoping for Junior selection were sharing indoor schools with Olympic riders and walking courses with them at build up events. As mentioned, Bertie had the likes of Mark Phillips, his sometimes underrated stable jockey, John Kersley, Hendrick Wiergersma, Stewart Stevens, and juniors such as Tony Hill and Alastair Martin-Bird. Bertie's daughter, Sarah, another Junior international, is married to racehorse trainer Philip Hobbs.

Rapscott was no place for the fainthearted, either on horseback or in poker games (and neither for blushing maidens). Replica Badminton fences would spring up on the farm and students would lay wagers and play dare. The

the early Fifties were the blossoming of Eventing the early Seventies were the start of another golden era. To ride at Badminton and Burghley standard it was of course possible to operate in a bit of a vacuum, or to find a shared guru as some of the late Sixties' riders did. Celia Ross

yard produced some of the most fearless riders of their generation.

Dick Stillwell, who as well as being a horseman had been involved in motor racing, ran a competition yard at Wokingham, near Reading. His main expertise was Show Jumping, and in later years had the sense to train both the Greek and Bermudan teams! He also, however, was greatly responsible for the success of Olympic three-time gold medallist, Richard Meade, and Olympic gold medallist, World and European Champion, Mary Gordon-Watson. Dick's indoor school was a fairly tight, dark place with hay bales up the side. His methods would give today's health and safety 'apparatchiks' heart failure. To make riders sit up straight he would shove a broom handle down their back, and to stop their legs flapping he would tie the stirrups to the girth of the saddle.

He was notorious for bumming cigarettes from clients' connections and would happily take a pee in the corner of the school while imparting some words of wisdom. It goes without saying that he was immensely popular and a very, very good horseman and imparter of knowledge.

At major events he would take very senior riders and his less experienced chicks on detailed course walks with legendary instructions: 'Lucinda, Richard, you two can go the short route...Minnie, don't you bloody go that way... Cowboys and Indians...You play safe.' He also held court in the 10-minute box during the long format days, dispensing wisdom to those who were about to take on the course. Dick would be glued to the closed circuit TV and watch how every fence was jumping and note any variations in ground conditions.

An old-school horseman, he was great to follow out hunting, and he could light a cigar while the horse under him was extricating itself from a fearsome bog, or jumping a five bar gate.

As might be expected of a yard run by a Swede, Waterstock House near Oxford was run on less carefree rein than Rapscott or Dick Stillwell's. Lars Sederholm was a leading trainer of horses in all disciplines and his yard also had a big Show Jumping angle. Lars, however, was the mentor for Badminton's youngest winner, Richard Walker, and Richard effectively became senior rider and star instructor at the yard in the early Seventies. Waterstock

Left: *Ken Clawson*

was another magnet for those wanting to join an elite stable squad heading for Badminton or Burghley, or the younger brigade, hoping to get selected for the Junior team and the final selection at Tidworth Three Day Event, the month after Badminton.

In the glory days a helicopter would arrive a few times a week, and former amateur steeplechase jockey and businessman, Chris Collins, would emerge for intense training to turn him into an international Three Day Event rider.

As a rider fitness exercise each evening about half a dozen horses would be cantered bareback round the school with just a head collar for steering. Future British team vet, Paul Farrington, would turn up on many an evening to take out the yard's head girl and future wife, Jo.

In those days it was very much a friendly contest at the big events between the Rapscott and Waterstock camps, with honours pretty evenly spread.

After Richard Walker left, Goran 'Yogi' Breisner became the star rider and coach at Waterstock and the Sederholm tradition became very influential when Yogi took over teaching the British team.

Right: *Lord and Lady Hugh Russell*

Far Right: *David Hunt*

Just a little bit later Alison Oliver, based near Windsor, found the limelight as the trainer, along with David Hunt, to turn Princess Anne into a European Eventing champion. Her yard also began to buzz with championship build up tension. Some of the inmates included the hilarious Irish international, Norman Van De Vater, and Lester Piggott's daughter, Maureen. There were some legendary parties at the Oliver yard and Alison continued producing top combinations from her base in Oxfordshire when she moved. Her top rider became Jonny Mc Irvine, whose estranged wife, Nicky, put

the surname on the Badminton Trophy before marrying Sebastian Coe.

Another Alison/David Hunt success was Sandy Pfleuger who came second at Badminton with Free Scott, to Mark Phillips, whom she would later marry.

There was little jealousy between yards and many riders went to specialists in different fields. One might be based, say, at Alison's, but have Dressage specials with David Hunt and have Cross Country pep ups with Dick. There were other discipline experts such as Pat Burgess who put people like Richard Meade through their Show Jumping paces, and non-riding genius trainers such as Dot Willis, who effectively produced Ginny Leng.

Some previously top riders like Celia Ross-Taylor, Brian Crago and Barbara Hammond took one or two younger riders under their wings, while persuading them to seek advice from many other sources, while Sheila Willcox knocked Mary Thomson (King) into shape.

Former Burghley winner, Gill Watson, for many years masterminded the difficult transition from Junior to Senior squads via Young Riders, and more recently Ruth McMullen has helped make Pippa Funnell. Ken Clawson was the Jumping guru for many of today's top stars and Tracie Robinson kept the Dressage up to scratch.

Bathampton House at Wylye in Wiltshire was the home of Lord and Lady Hugh Russell. Both Hugh, brother of the Duke of Bedford, and Rosemary Russell were keen amateurs and rode at the big events in the early days. At their undulating estate she designed practice versions in different sizes of every imaginable type of Cross Country jump. She would hold Cross Country sessions for many of the great and good of the

Right: *Alison Oliver and Lars Sederholm*

sport, including Lucinda Prior-Palmer (Green) and Sue Hatherly (Benson). Much of what Sue learnt at Wylye will have given her the confidence to design the Cross Country course for the Greenwich Olympics.

Rosemary would hurtle about the fields barking instructions from her Mini Moke vehicle, generally putting the wind up some of the world's most senior riders.

Like many a centre Wylye hosted courses taken by the likes of Dick Stillwell. These were fantastic opportunities and, again, less experienced riders were there with people like Jane Holderness-Roddam. Rosemary loved good food and had some superb cooks to look after the riders, and even provided grooms for one or two cheeky younger riders who requested them.

For many years until the Russells sold

up to move to Wales, Wylye was where the British team went to concentrate before the Olympic, World and European Championships. At the big events Rosemary would inevitably be there with the Moke, and a rider knew they had arrived if they were part of the Moke 'set'.

There has always been some glamour having a foreign guru, and this has been two-way traffic. Mark Phillips trained the US team for over 20 years, Ginny Leng had a stint with the Irish, and arguably the most successful has been British former Badminton winner and international Dressage rider, Chris Bartle, who became trainer for the German team and, had it not been for Bettina Hoy's elimination for circling after the bell at Athens, would have presided over an Olympic clean sweep on three occasions.

Momentous Changes

Far Right: *Roads and Tracks*

The rules of Eventing are forever changing both nationally and internationally, but there have been some which have changed the very nature of the sport.

In the section about the history and origins of horse trials, we showed how many formats were tried out in the early days, but how it basically settled into this shape: Day one: Dressage. Day two: Endurance, encompassing Roads and Tracks to Steeplechase to Roads and Tracks to 10-minute break to Cross Country (and originally with a warm down run in). Day three: Show Jumping.

It was originally only open to military officers, hence dubious promotions of 'other ranks' to officer class to be eligible,

as at Berlin. It was still something of a novelty that Sergeant Ben Jones was part of Britain's gold medal team at the Mexico Olympics.

Women could ride at Badminton and Harewood, though not at the Olympics until Lana Du Pont broke the mould. Since, females such as Vivian Machin-Goodall, fifth at the first Badminton, through Sheila Willcox to Jane Bullen, Lucinda Prior-Palmer, Ginny Leng, Mary King and Pippa Funnell, to name just some, have shown that they are every bit as good as the men.

There used to be a minimum weight to carry on the Endurance phases of 11 stone 11 pounds, with the girls needing weight cloths to get to make the scales. Considering how horse racing is strictly

LITTLE BOOK OF **EVENTING**

based on weights for handicaps, which would suggest that weight is an enormous influence, Eventing decided to take all weight requirements out of the equation in 1998, reasoning that the 'dead' lead weight for the girls (and lighter men such as World Champion, Blyth Tait) put them at a disadvantage to the moving weight of the heavier men. This move surprisingly seemed uncontroversial, despite the racing analogy.

There used to be something called penalty zones, which were pegged some yards in front of a Cross Country jump at Three Day Events and further on the landing side, the idea being that any penalisable offence had to take place in this 'box'. In other words, if a horse put on the brakes outside the zone, but was shoved into action over the jump, despite the disobedience being attributable to the jump, they would be clear. Likewise, if a rider was dislodged going over the jump, if they could hang on until they were out of the zone before putting their feet on the ground, they would get away with no 60 penalties for a fall. There were some heroic and crowd pleasing efforts, and now riders are required to retire after a fall if it has any connection with the fence.

With a sport where endurance and a certain amount of biffs and bashes were inevitable, for many years the 'equine Aspirin', Bute, was permitted to be administered to horses to keep them sound for the Show Jumping day. Though the ethos of the sport has always been that horse welfare is paramount, and the element of preservation for the final day an integral part of the sport (unlike, say, racing), many felt that a mild pain relief sachet was well within the spirit of the competition. Indeed the career of many an old and experienced horse was probable extended by several years by the use of Bute.

Others disagreed and took the purist view that if the horse needed ANY masking of lameness the rider had failed the test of horsemanship. There were vociferous debates at the time, one even taking place in the hallowed Oxford Union.

Bute was banned in 1989 and the whole Endurance aspect of the sport was beginning its decline in influence. The Roads and Tracks became shorter and shorter and as horses became more expensive, and riders more professional, the desire to run them at a 'Major' more than twice a year grew.

With riders becoming full time Eventers, with very few one-horse amateurs getting a look in at the big events, the problem for the big players is how to keep their owners happy.

If the stars run yards like racing stables, with multiple horses, but with the equivalent situation of the owners expecting the trainer to ride in all the top races, a difficult situation arises.

The long ago Bute ban was the first nail in the coffin of the traditional Three Day Event, which culminated in the whole Endurance phase being ditched in 2006. In fairness, the paying public wouldn't spot the difference as the Roads and Tracks and 'Chase were not part of the spectator experience, but Eventing was ever a participant sport, and the sense of achievement in doing the long haul of the past has now been diminished. The idea, of course, was to increase the inclusion zone of participating countries, though a look at the very broad base of the entries at the long format 1948 Olympics might suggest that there might have been a downside to the UK taking over the Eventing world that seemed to freeze out more exotic nations. Now the sport could be accused of patronising the equestrian world by bringing down the standard to accommodate newcomers.

The Cross Country phase was what totally distinguished Eventing from pure Dressage and pure Show Jumping, and its influence was much greater than now. In fairness, the standard of Dressage and Jumping in Eventing has improved enormously, but the balance of influence has all changed.

The big events now celebrate their multinational entries, which is fine, but there is a reason that riders from Jamaica and Thailand, Croatia and Bermuda are now able to take part. The big ones no longer frighten them off.

The sport is much more pro now, which has its advantages, but a link to its heritage is important, otherwise it has no point. Hopefully this book will enlighten some new enthusiasts to why exactly they are actually involved in the sport they have chosen to follow.

There have been dark days of the sport, when in a short time span several riders were killed. Suffice it to say that ironically in the days of really scary jumps, less well constructed and with no ground lines and massive drops, in April mud and a gung ho amateurism, very few horses and no riders were killed.

There was a terrible spate of rider deaths in the 1990s and inevitably all sorts of measures were looked at. One of the most constructive of these has been

the introduction of something called a Frangible Pin. These can be used on upright wooden fences like post and rails or gates and will safely collapse the fence if hit really hard. This will stop the lethal rotational falls where the horse falls on the rider.

Course designers had for many years been encouraged to put very time consuming smaller versions of the jumps that would allow completion for the less experienced but reward the brave. With the old idea that any route between the red flags on the right and white on the left was acceptable, course builders had to erect great artistic barriers joining the longer and shorter routes. This was commonly known as 'Sexy Fencing'. It looked nice but cost a fortune. Sense prevailed with the 'black flag rule'. This really meant a black strip on one of the marker flags to designate it as an alternative. No more sexy fencing needed, but slight confusion for the spectators as the blanket 'red right, white left' went out of the window.

Author's note. The sport having continental origins is why the red flag is on the right and white on the left. Driving on the right of the road you would follow the red rear lights and the white headlights would come at you from the left. See, a reason for everything!

The Jumps

There was pure Dressage with elegant and even dangerous manoeuvres, and Show Jumping over knock down, coloured and decorated jumps, but the one thing that made Eventing unique was the Cross Country Jumping tests.

These fences were solid obstacles which were replicas of a true line out hunting or the test of the rider courier 'Who got through or died.'

Xenophon was right to realise that a good army needed to cross all sorts of terrain. The Cross Country courses in the Eventing world have reflected this over the years, but have adapted to the times.

It was perfectly normal for the 10th Duke of Beaufort to test out fences at the early Badmintons on a hunter, as the test of confidence of horse and rider would be very similar to an unseen obstruction in the way of following hounds.

It was clever of the first Eventing course designers to try and emulate the experience. In the early days the jumps were made of relatively flimsy timber, 'found' on the farms and estates that hosted early trials.

Each course would try to feature as many natural obstacles that would happily sit in the available landscape.

Hills were useful, ditches a boon and if there was any type of pond, it had to be brought into play. Stone walls, hedges, five bar gates and farm paraphernalia, like sheep or pheasant feeders, were

designated as jumps.

Any ideas seen on the Continent were happily borrowed.

Here are some of the standard types of jump before the more sophisticated kind of obstacle came into play. All courses from training level to Badminton should start with one or two confidence building, relatively easy fences. When Three Day Eventing had the Endurance phases of Roads and Tracks and Steeplechase, riders and horses would have had a spin round the easy 'chase' jumps, albeit at a faster pace than needed

for Cross Country. At least the blood was up.

With the regular One Day Event scene the Cross Country is the last phase (totally ignoring the old premise of saving some of your horse for the next bit).

The basic ingredients of Cross Country fences are fir poles, railway sleepers, dry stone walls, spruce hedges, straw bales, petrol barrels and a good imagination. With an increase of sophistication joined up jumps, or combinations were introduced.

Above: *Barrels*

The illustrations decorating the pages of this book are from events which range from the Pony Club Championships to the Windsor Three Day Event and the British Open at Gatcombe Park. The level of difficulty is not so much based on height (which for Olympic level hasn't really changed since 1912) but that surprisingly, the height difference between the two, is only five inches.

It is where the jumps are placed and designed that makes all the difference. Something that looks really scary to a spectator, and indeed a nervous competitor, could in fact be really quite easy for a horse to jump. Equally some of the really 'clever' conundrum jumps, built to test riders who have honed their skills over 30 years, can look rather boring to the spectating public.

The first jumps were just single obstacles in places that fitted the parks and farms. Early examples tended to have flimsy poles and very undefined ground lines. Many early One Day Event courses resembled Hunter Trial courses which were indeed the precursors to the real event course. On some of the Hunter Trial tracks riders were required to stop and open, then shut a gate. Though there was an optimum time,

this was kept secret from the riders. It was known as the 'bogey time' and it was up to the riders to judge a decent pace. This approach is so very different from the minute markers top riders plot on their routes with their state of the art stopwatches.

Even at the early big Three Day Events the jumps were very natural and rustic looking. Despite the rules on dimensions the outlook of the main competition jumps has altered a lot over the years. Some of the early courses had jumps that would look positively simple to the sophisticates of today, but likewise, some of the spindly timber, no ground line, offerings of the early days, look quite unjumpable. Equally, some of the 'scaries' of the middle years look much more of a challenge than recent examples. Just note the difference in the drop fence at the LA Olympics, compared to its equivalent at Greenwich 28 years later.

Now riders expect to get round. Then it was horse against course and if you had

a refusal you certainly had your three goes before you had to call it a day. Same with falls. There was always the adage that there were fools, damn fools and men who remounted in Steeplechases. In Eventing remounting after a crashing fall was a point of honour and on some occasions actually contributed to gold medals.

Now after a stop a rider is expected to retire, and indeed the rules state they must after a fall.

The main need to be able to jump obstacles across country really came with the enclosure acts and the golden age of foxhunting. Initially these runs inspired Steeplechase racing, literally wager races from one steeple to the next. These became end of season hunting jollies when riders rode from one point to another, taking their own root. Hence Point to Point racing. Some hunts still have annual hunt rides over natural country, since Point to Pointing has become recently much more quasi professional racing.

Famous fences that have developed and been reproduced in imitation forms include:

The Coffin: This title is slightly misleading as what it consist of is a post

and rail, down a slope to a grave-like ditch, then up a slope to another post and rail.

The Irish Bank: Usually over a ditch to a grassed bank, which the horses are expected to touch down on before jumping a ditch away. The modern versions have logs on the top and narrow approach fences. As natural obstacles they would be found in many an Irish Hunt country.

The Cornish Bank: Not seen for some years, but similar to the Irish Bank, but with a dry stone wall facing. Again, horses are expected to touch down on top.

The Pheasant Feeder: Something you might meet in a wooded part of the course. A small, roofed hut.

The Lamb Feeder: These would usually be stuck out in a field where their inspiration would sit. They consist of parallel bars, with little or no ground line.

The Log Pile: Somewhat self-explanatory, but could be surprisingly

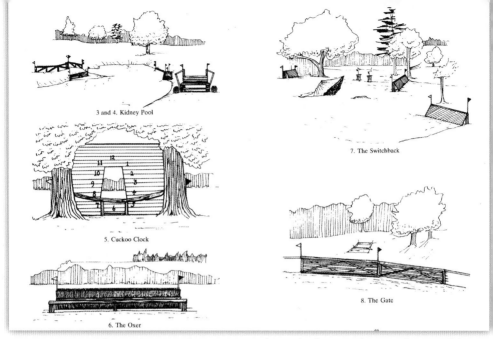

3 and 4. Kidney Pool

7. The Switchback

5. Cuckoo Clock

8. The Gate

6. The Oxer

Above: *A variety of jumps*

wide to impress the spectators, but usually what would be considered as a let up fence.

The Bounce: A double jump where there is no room to put a horse's stride between the two, so the horse has to land and take straight off again. These were taken a stage or two further, with double bounces, or bounces into water.

Into Space: A jump with an innocuous take-off but a leap down a drop. Less in fashion than they used to be, since they were thought to put too much strain on

the horses. The most famous of these is not at a Horse Trial, but Bechers Brook on the Grand National racecourse at Aintree. Even that has been modified out of recognition by the safety brigade. The Normandy Bank at Badminton and the Leaf Pit at Burghley are the best Eventing examples. In early Grand Nationals there was a stone wall in front of the grandstand, and Captain Becher really did fall into the brook named after him.

The Hay Bales: Another 'found' jump

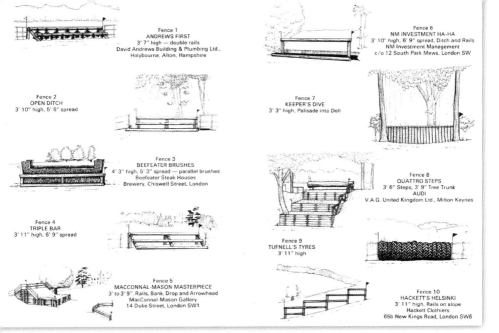

Fence 1
ANDREWS FIRST
3' 7" high — double rails
David Andrews Building & Plumbing Ltd.,
Holybourne, Alton, Hampshire

Fence 2
OPEN DITCH
3' 10" high, 5' 6" spread

Fence 3
BEEFEATER BRUSHES
4' 3" high, 5' 3" spread — parallel brushes
Beefeater Steak Houses
Brewery, Chiswell Street, London

Fence 4
TRIPLE BAR
3' 11" high, 6' 9" spread

Fence 5
MACCONNAL-MASON MASTERPIECE
3' to 3' 9". Rails, Bank, Drop and Arrowhead
MacConnal-Mason Gallery
14 Duke Street, London SW1

Fence 6
NM INVESTMENT HA-HA
3' 10" high, 6' 9" spread, Ditch and Rails
NM Investment Management
c/o 12 South Park Mews, London SW

Fence 7
KEEPER'S DIVE
3' 3" high, Palisade into Dell

Fence 8
QUATTRO STEPS
3' 6" Steps, 3' 9" Tree Trunk
AUDI
V.A.G. United Kingdom Ltd., Milton Keynes

Fence 9
TUFNELL'S TYRES
3' 11" high

Fence 10
HACKETT'S HELSINKI
3' 11" high, Rails on slope
Hackett Clothiers
65b New Kings Road, London SW6

Above: *A variety of fences*

out in the countryside, usually beefed up with some timber poles.

Sponsor-inspired jumps: At Badminton there were some genuine beer Drays when the event was sponsored by brewers, Whitbread. In the Mitsubishi days horses leaped two backed up Mitsubishi pickup trucks. At a one-off event in America horses jumped the bonnet of a Rolls-Royce. One small clip from a hoof cost five figures to repair. Not repeated.

Whitbread also had a stack of beer barrels and a pub bar to jump, which for several years had a roof.

Ha Ha: Many big estates that host events have ha has, a walled drop from the smart part of the park to the farm bit, and these made a natural obstacle. These could easily be converted to involve large brush drops, as seen at Burghley.

Stone Walls: These are found in many parks and are useful natural barriers to be jumped between enclosures.

Arrowheads: Quite a new invention in the days of high accuracy riding.

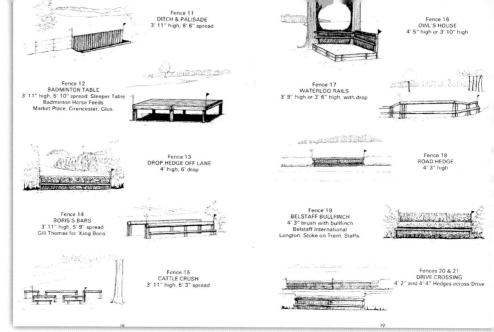

Above: *Even more jumps and fences*

Fence 11
DITCH & PALISADE
3' 11" high, 6' 6" spread

Fence 12
BADMINTON TABLE
3' 11" high, 5' 10" spread. Sleeper Table
Badminton Horse Feeds
Market Place, Cirencester, Glos.

Fence 13
DROP HEDGE OFF LANE
4' high, 6' drop

Fence 14
BORIS'S BARS
3' 11" high, 5' 9" spread
Gill Thomas for 'King Boris'

Fence 15
CATTLE CRUSH
3' 11" high, 5' 3" spread

Fence 16
OWL'S HOUSE
4' 5" high or 3' 10" high

Fence 17
WATERLOO RAILS
3' 9" high or 3' 6" high, with drop

Fence 18
ROAD HEDGE
4' 3" high

Fence 19
BELSTAFF BULLFINCH
4' 3" brush with bullfinch
Belstaff International
Longton, Stoke on Trent, Staffs.

Fences 20 & 21
DRIVE CROSSING
4' 2" and 4' 4" Hedges across Drive

They are now known generically as 'Skinnies' and often come after a jump that requires an extravagant effort, to test rider control. These can also look like toadstools or mini 'Hitler moustache' brushes.

Bullfinch: Another old-fashioned jump which came from the hunting field. These are quite soft brush jumps but up to 10 feet high. The idea is for the horse to trust the rider enough to burst through the fronds, not seeing where it is going.

Roll Tops: These are part of the new trend of portable jump which can be plonked anywhere on a park and put at clever angles. As individual components they are pretty harmless, but their placing is all.

Five Bar Gate: These used to be exactly as described, fully upright with no ground line. They would be a good steady up call for riders halfway round a freewheeling course. Now gates obstacles tend to have chunky rocks as a ground line and are either sloped or semi-collapsible.

Steeplechase jumps: These are as described, but nice let off jumps either at the start or halfway round a track.

Many of these Eventing course ideas came from the pre-war Hunter Trials. There was one in the Grafton Hunt country near Greens Norton, Northamptonshire, started by Colonel V.D.S. Williams, father of the well known equestrian commentator, Dorian Williams. The Grafton Trials were known as the Grand National of Hunter Trials and were written up in an equestrian annual, *The Horseman's Year 1946-1947*, interestingly just before the Aldershot Olympic Trials and the following first Badminton.

A section on Hunter Trials in the book gives some useful tips to those thinking of running one of these contests, which were designed, like Point to Points, as hunt fundraisers.

"HUNTER TRIALS: These are probably the easiest to make attractive to the competitor and the most difficult to keep interesting for the spectators."

(Badminton and Burghley crowds would now suggest that the spectators keep very interested!)

"They can be held either in the autumn or the spring, the latter is probably preferable as horses are fit and riders in more of a jumping mood than after a summer's inactivity. The best time is probably a week or ten days after the last day's hunting, but of course it is difficult to forecast. If held in the autumn they should be held in the latter half of October.

They should be designed to test all the qualities that are required of the first-class hunter in the particular district in which they are held, and to try to select the horse that is most likely to carry an average horseman well over normal country rather than one which, in the hands of an expert, can negotiate a series of outsize obstacles."

This would be a reasonable description of a novice level course today. Some current Cross Country course designers might like to reflect on the type of natural obstacle needed for a true 'Cross Country' test, in this day of contrived, over-decorated portable fences, sometimes just plonked in the middle of a field with no context.

"The types of obstacle must obviously vary in different districts in which these trials are held, but the broad principles remain the same. Fences should be as natural as possible, but if it is necessary to make artificial ones, they should be built into existing fences and not put out in the middle of a field with wings;...the first few should be comparatively easy to give the genuine hunter, not used to jumping in cold blood, a chance to warm up.

A cut and laid fence about three feet high is suitable to start with, followed by a post and rails about the same height. Next perhaps a cut and laid fence with a ditch away from it, after which the more difficult fences can be met in any order that the lie of the land makes suitable. These should include, if possible, a fence with a ditch in front of it, a larger post and rails with or without a ditch and varying height from three feet six inches for novice and local classes and to four feet for Championships."

(These dimensions are not far off the rules even now for events as big as Badminton, though placing and terrain make all the difference).

"...a gate to jump, water to be cramped on the way out and flown on the way home."

Here Hunter Trials differ from event courses.

"...followed by a gate within fifty yards of it that competitors have to open. The size of the water must depend on the natural brook, but ten feet is quite enough to cause alarm and consternation among riders until they have ridden over it and most of them, found how easy it is. If there is a lane on the course it can be negotiated twice, once directly in and out and the other with slip rails into it, trot along it about fifty yards and jump out. In any case a fence should be arranged which has to be jumped with only a short run. The remainder of the fences can be repetitions or variations of the above. In districts where walls, banks etc. are commonly met, these should of course be included."

Modern course builders will 'borrow' ideas from not just other hunt countries, but events in other actual countries. (Cf. The Normandy Bank, Irish Bank, Horsens Bridge, the Taxis etc.)

The Grafton course was genuinely formidable as the map and picture of the open water show.

Today event courses at all levels have moved on a long way from the Hunter Trials of old, but designers should try to keep the ethos of a genuinely Cross Country adventure and not create a long distance Show Jumping track.

Weird Ones

Far Right: *Flood conditions in Mexico*

There have been some strange incidents over the years at events. For example, one year at Badminton at a jump with a big log over a gaping ditch called the Stockholm Fence, a horse, Gurgle the Greek, ridden by Rachel Bayliss, looked as if he had slid to a refusal, but Rachel kept urging Gurgle on as they slipped into the ditch, and they emerged unscathed and un-penalised the other side. The rules stating that as they had gone through the red flag on the right and the white on the left, without parting company, they were clear. The rules and indeed fence design now make a repeat of that trick a one-off.

At Tidworth during the Roads and Tracks phase, high on a windy ridge on Salisbury Plain a rider, Vicky Spencer-Cox, and her horse were struck by lightning. The horse was killed and Vicky knocked unconscious.

Riding a strong horse at Badminton Australian rider, Stuart Tinney, jumped the obstacle coming out of the Lake, but the horse saw what it thought was a gap in the crowd, actually a largely seated crowd as it was the designated disabled viewing area, and launched over the barrier and into the spectators, knocking to the ground an American documentary film maker.

Glamour model, Katie Price, who was at Badminton to promote her range of bright pink riding wear, mistook the welcome she had been afforded at the

event by settling into a seat in the Royal Box to watch the Show Jumping, before being politely asked to move along.

One year at Badminton a security team spotted a suspicious package up a tree near a Cross Country jump. The bomb squad were scrambled by chopper, until it was discovered that the package was in fact an unauthorised camera remote, placed by an unofficial photographer, but welcome eccentric, 'Gypsy Joe'.

Mark Todd set off round Burghley with Bertie Blunt with a real chance of winning, having not been informed that he had missed a compulsory flag on the Roads and Tracks, and thus been eliminated. Not surprisingly he and the horse's connections were cross that they had risked the Cross Country for nothing.

The Duke of Beaufort, Badminton Director, Hugh Thomas, and TV commentator, Mike Tucker, have all come second at Badminton.

Even the Dressage arena is not a place immune to disasters. Leaving the arena results in elimination and this has happened at Badminton. On another occasion a rider's top hat came off as he was doing an extended trot diagonally across the arena and landed on X. The next movement was to extend back across the other diagonal. The rider took aim and bravely trashed his £200 headgear on the return run.

At the Open Championships, when they were held at Goodwood in Sussex, one rider with close connections to this chapter, had qualified a great Cross Country horse, who was always a bit of a handful in the Dressage. At Goodwood the arena was sand, but the outer rim mown grass. The weather was atrocious with rain coming down in stair rods. As the arena was sand the rider hadn't thought to put studs in the horse's shoes.

The start bell rang, indicating a countdown to entering the arena. The rider launched into the required canter down the side of the arena and turned sharp left to make his triumphant entrance. On the turn the studless horse skidded on to its side, depositing the jockey. One whole side of the horse was covered in mud, as was half of the rider's elegant clothing.

The clock was still ticking. A friendly member of the crowd legged the rider back into the saddle.

Unfortunately the rein had broken about six inches from the bit on one side with about six feet on the other. The helper tied them in a knot and our hero entered the arena in the nick of time and lurched to a halt at X. The senior judge was one of the scariest on the circuit. A smile was not forthcoming as the rider saluted and jammed his hat back on.

Disaster. The knot had come undone. Too late for running repairs and not about to let this minor inconvenience disqualify the pair, the rider, looking forward to a good Cross Country spin, leaned forward, grabbed the six inches in one hand and wrapped the spare six feet round the other and proceeded to steer through an approximation of the test.

By some miracle, seven minutes later the combination came back up the centre line to take their bow.

The crowd was charmingly appreciative. The scary judge left the shelter of her warm car, came out into the elements, walked up to the rider and said she was going to report him for bringing the sport into disrepute.

They had a fantastic Cross Country round.

At the Mexico Olympics in 1968 there was a flash flood on Cross Country day. Some of the fences were literally invisible, only marked out by their flags.

Thirty of the 49 starters had completed, so most in touch teams had managed to get at least three round before the heavens opened. Ironically the two horse fatalities occurred before the rain. There were six jumps which crossed a brook, and of course it was here that the rising tide broke the banks and turned what had been a three-metre spread into an undefined 12 metres. The competition carried on regardless and was probably the most extreme event ever experienced.

At the same event the Russian rider, going for the individual gold medal in the Show Jumping phase, took the wrong course and was eliminated.

Richard Meade, riding last to win Badminton went so slowly to jump clear that he obtained time faults and dropped to second.

Bettina Hoy was all set to win the individual gold at Athens and after the bell rang in the Show Jumping phase she went through the start. Then, for no fathomable reason, she looped back through the starting gate before jumping clear. She was presented with the gold medal, but an objection that she had broken the rules was eventually upheld and many weeks after the event she was disqualified.

Media

In the pre-war era of hunting, racing and polo, all three of which were covered in the national press, Eventing didn't get a look in. When the first Badminton, however, announced itself as "The Most Important Horse Event in Great Britain" there became a certain, curious interest. Equestrian sport received a big boost at Helsinki three years later when Harry Llewellyn won the Show Jumping gold with Foxhunter, and the Badminton crowds got bigger and bigger as the years went on.

Though it has always been a technical challenge to achieve, Badminton was televised from 1954, and remains one of the corporation's big outside broadcasts.

The picture papers recorded Royal visits to the Trials and Badminton was the place where her Majesty and her party mingled in a relaxed manner amongst the public.

The sport suddenly went big when Princess Anne became European Champion at Burghley in 1971. Of course the downside to this was that what had quietly been a rural upmarket interest instantly became the sport that in media land required one to be Royal, or nearly, to be involved. This did at least put Eventing on the front pages, but secured the elitist image.

The paparazzi turned up in force

LITTLE BOOK OF **EVENTING**

and there were *Giles* cartoons in the papers and *Private Eye* spoofs. Badminton took on local journalist, Jim Gilmore, as Press Officer to cope with the brouhaha.

Nowadays there is so much spread in media outlets that both sport HQ at British Eventing and all the major events not only deal with the old forms of press such as national, local and equestrian media but documentary crews, radio syndicated interviews, Facebook, YouTube, and Twitter.

Top events sometimes have dedicated radio stations, and personal headphones can be bought on the day. These give commentary and interviews with riders and other top people involved with the event. Also, this is a useful, limited radius broadcast which drivers can pick up in their cars as they make their way to the event and hear traffic reports.

The TV coverage is syndicated and re-edited for distribution around the world and in Olympic years there can be as many as 14 TV crews in operation at an event such as Badminton.

When Zara Phillips hit the scene the whole media thing kicked off again with unrealistic speculation that she would ride at the Athens Games and then at Hong Kong. The truth is that this was never on the cards, but then, with the cancellation of Badminton 2012, which would have been a make or break selection trial, the selectors took a punt and included her in the team for Greenwich.

This was a fantastic opportunity for media coverage. The Eventing was the first of the four sports to take place at Greenwich, (Modern Pentathlon wrapped the Games), and was considered 'a risk' by the top powers that be. This meant that any injury of horse or rider could have presented a media flurry. Right at the start of the Games, with a Royal rider, and animal welfare to the fore, Greenwich, and indeed the whole Games, didn't need a disaster. Luck always plays a part, but, as the cliché goes, you make your own luck, and the organisation did absolutely everything to make sure that the Cross Country ran as safely as it could in what is accepted as a risk sport.

The Royal rider certainly put the sport well on the map again, and

Far Left:
Dedicated radio station

the Greenwich Press Centre, fairly sensibly predicting before Zara's selection, a potential 200 journalists, was invaded by twice that number, and a dozen Royal spectators.

The Press room had photographers huddled on the floor filing their pics. They did not realise that the riders' and owners' hospitality area, where Royals came and went, was in full view!

TV coverage is the great pull for sponsors and even in these multi-channel days there is some kudos in getting your event on a terrestrial channel.

Now that everyone has access to a phone camera, the exclusivity of action shots is now a grey area for copyright purposes. However, main TV companies have covered the sport well despite the relative costs and complications of a long distance outside broadcast.

The BBC was the first in at Badminton, but over the years ITV has covered the sport regionally with Yorkshire TV doing Bramham and Meridian doing a series of southern events which included Windsor and Blenheim Three Days, and One Days at Lulworth Castle and the setting for

Downton Abbey, Highclere Castle. Sky TV has also covered some events.

Abroad, several companies make programmes and syndicate them to national broadcasters, and the International Federation, the FEI, has its own TV arm which makes online, subscription programmes for all the equestrian sports. In Britain there is a dedicated channel, Horse and Country TV.

Today, as filming is easier and cheaper, many more moving picture outlets are available for the sport, although the viewer numbers are naturally divided today by the vast choice of programmes.

Getting media attention in a crowded market is hard, especially when football reigns supreme, but niche broadcasting of popular, but minority sports, which today must include horse racing, have many loyal followers.

After the great success of the Greenwich Games, horse sports can promote themselves as not just a fantastic spectator experience, but something which at a lower level is not beyond the reach of a weekend amateur rider.

Sponsorship

In the early days of the sport, Eventing was a military underwritten training exercise or part of an Olympic Games. Then, with the first Badminton, an event needed to be solvent, or at least try to break even. As mentioned previously, the sport could not exist, even today, without a vast army of volunteers or some backing from a central organising body such as the British Horse Society (BHS) or the Federation Equestre International (FEI), or more recently on local level, British Eventing (BE).

From the early days Badminton's crowds kept going up and up, so box office then, as now, was a vital part of the event solvency. The smaller events were run for the riders, often as a guest invitation to a private estate. In the world of large estates which often hosted these competitions, commercialism was perhaps discreetly frowned upon.

This couldn't really remain sustainable and the blue chip image of the sport was rather a good place to subtly promote a company. The brewers, Whitbread, were the first company to sponsor a major horse race, and in the early Sixties Colonel Whitbread, a hunting friend of the 10th Duke of Beaufort, suggested his company might like to 'help' Badminton. For several years this sponsorship was so low key as to be almost under the radar.

Right: *Midland Bank*

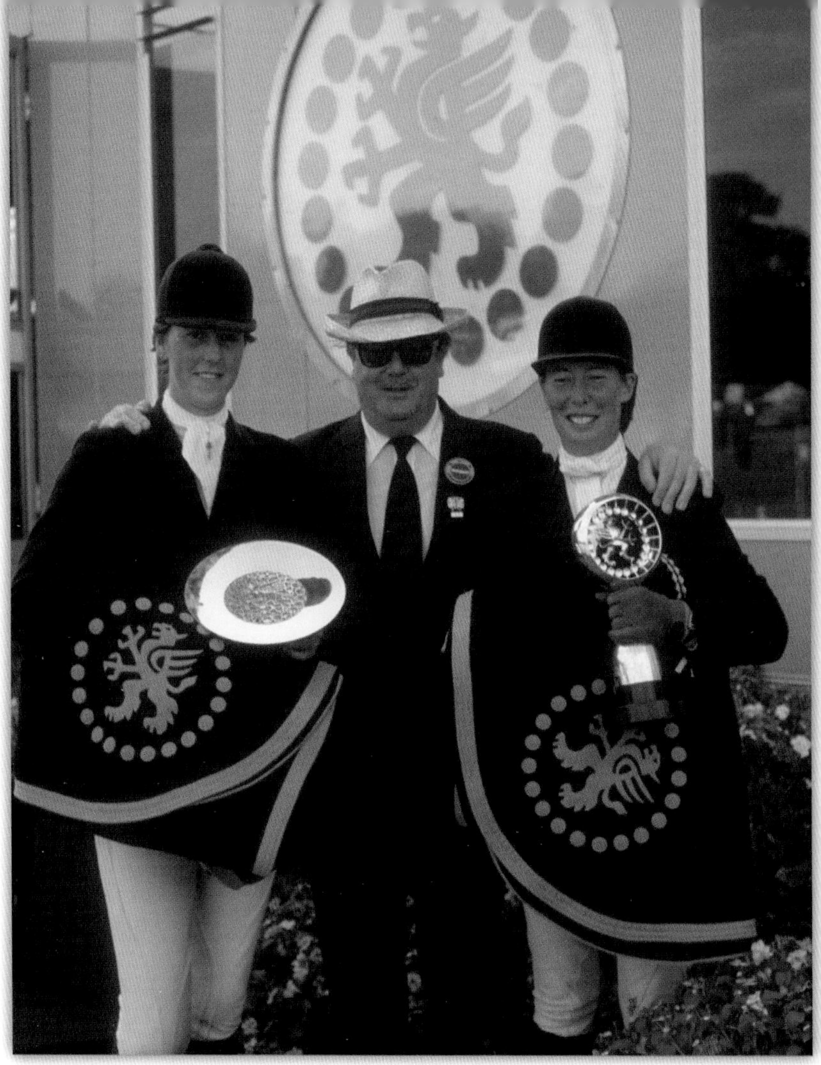

In their time Whitbread's sponsorship of the race and event were the longest in sport. Badminton's subsequent relationship with Mitsubishi enjoys an equally lasting, symbiotic match.

For the top events there is something wonderful to 'sell' a prospective sponsor. Fantastic setting, big crowd, TV coverage in a sport where cherished animals compete in thrilling contest with brave riders of both sexes, with what advertisers would deem an AB demographic following. The perception of elitism, which is to an extent misplaced today, actually does no harm in attracting top range sponsorship.

Horse sports will never have the popular appeal of football, a game which any kid anywhere in the world can aspire to, or golf, which has a massive, if higher social profile. They can, however, be great marketing targets for specific brands.

It is no surprise that the off road vehicle market has been very involved with the sport. It is in keeping that Rolex has an interest. This, however, has been at the showcase events.

For the whole sport in Britain, however, it was the Midland Bank who became the blanket sponsor of all events apart from the 'Majors', and were effectively instrumental in the sport really taking root. The One Day finals were known as the Midland Bank Championships, but all the nationwide qualifiers had branded yellow and black rosettes, which were more coveted than the rather paltry winners' cheques. In the early days riders were known to frame the cheques alongside the rosettes instead of cashing them.

This is where we come to the potential split in the sport between professionalisation and the Corinthian concept. Most riders, even at the top level, did it as a hobby and expected to pay for the fun of competing. It would not occur that they should be making a living from it.

It wasn't a hundred years ago that to play at Wimbledon the competitors had to be amateur, and in Rugby Union that distinction is even more recent.

Eventing costs money to put on and costs money to do. It still does, and unless a rider is in the minute clique at the top, the prizes do not make it viable.

Hence in the late Seventies riders

started looking for commercial support. The idea that 'trade' was socially unacceptable in what had been perceived as a 'posh' sport was somewhat blown out of the water when the first 'flashy' pantechnicon of a horsebox, with advertising on the side, rocked up at the start of the season. The driver had the telltale personal registration number ANN 1.

Specific rider sponsorship is still with us, but it never really took off as a concept, and the racing model of supportive ownership is still more of the norm for individuals.

Eventing in Britain, which under the auspices of the Midland Bank, had truly become the centre of the world, had something of a hiatus when they no longer had their regional target (they are now part of HSBC) and withdrew from the sport altogether.

The first independents to back a horse trial were an eclectic joint venture of a sweets company and a Mayfair art gallery, hence the Alma, McConnell-Mason events. Suddenly the ubiquitous tweed and flat cap dress code was invaded by branded blousons and baseball caps. 'Pass the smelling salts Dorothy'. At the Greenwich Olympics

Left: *Rolex*

30 years later the performance director of team GBR, a former Commanding Officer of the King's Troop RHA, was so corporately garbed that he could have been flipping burgers! (as indeed could the Games Makers).

Each event was now on its own to find some sort of backing and many survived by relying on local companies to sponsor individual jumps, in return for a decent mention on the tannoy system.

On the whole the big British events still attract a title sponsor, as indeed does Kentucky with Rolex in the USA, whereas on the Continent they tend to have multiple supporters.

Rolex came up with a good idea for a super prize of $250.00 for a rider when they devised a three in a row challenge to win Badminton, Burghley and Rolex consecutively, in any order and on any three horses. (This was invented in Long Format days when with Badminton and Rolex a weekend apart the same horse running at both couldn't happen. With a calendar blip giving a two-week break in Short Format it might just be possible to do all three on the same horse, though very unlikely anyone would try). It has

only been won once.

For a few years HSBC came up with an accumulator of points won at just the four star internationals, with a big $100,000 annual prize. This so favoured the tiny bunch of multiple horse-riding stars that only about five people were ever in the running, and this created an unnatural apartheid not just between the top pro riders and the lower level full timers, which is the norm in most sports from football and golf to motor racing and tennis, but between a tiny minority and the others equally at the top of their sport.

There is still a slightly uneasy balance between a sport which is still amateur in approach (ie needing a vast number of volunteers to exist) and a top level that still rankles that their prizes don't match that of some other sports.

Whether as the backer of an up and coming rider, or a fence sponsor at a minor event, to the big players, such as Mitsubishi, Land Rover, Rolex and HSBC, the sport of Eventing does have a great many things going for it, and it is no surprise that it retains volunteers, officials, fans and sponsors for very long periods, and punches well above its weight for loyalty adherence.

Far Left:
Mitsubishi Motors

Right: *Land Rover*

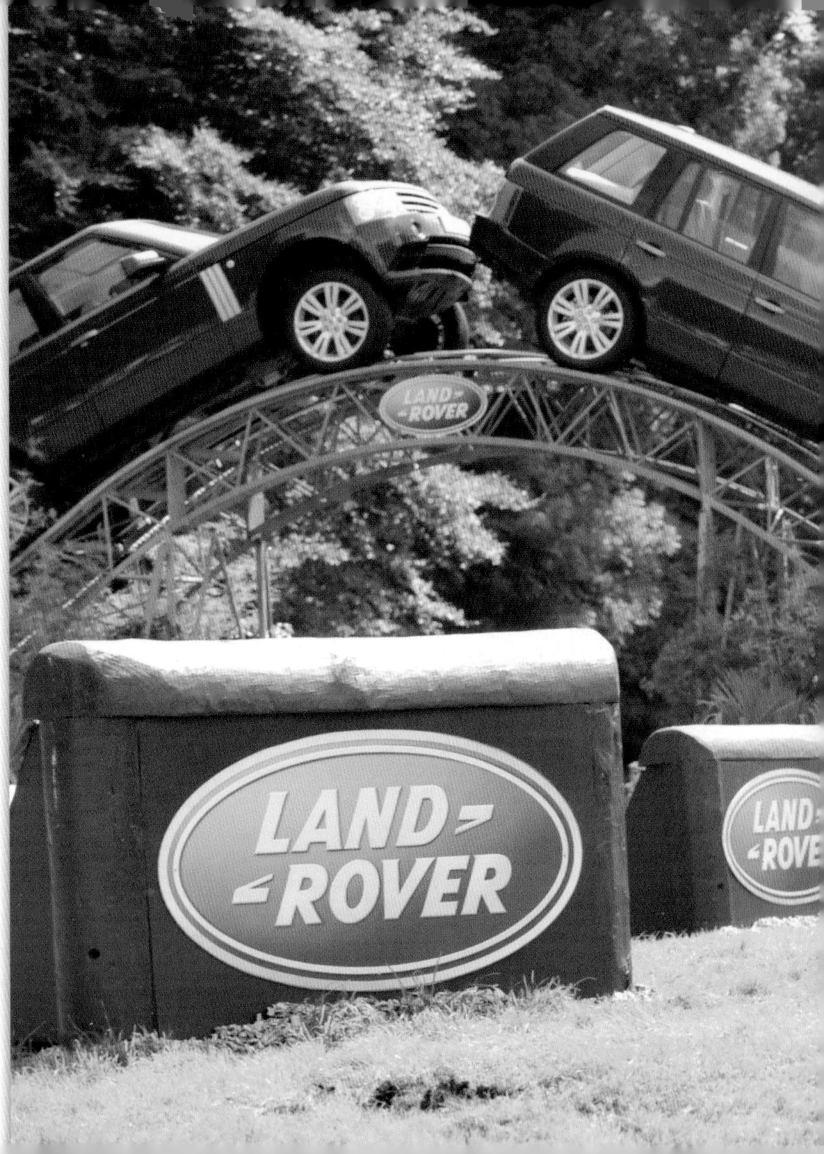

Be Involved

As I wrote many years ago in *Sixteen Hands Between Your Legs*, you don't have to have ambitions to become an international rider to enjoy one of the most friendly sports around. I'm sure there are many merits to being a swimming or athletics groupie. Tennis mums and soccer dads must love traipsing around in pursuit of their kids' glory, but must surely melt away when the dream has been achieved or dashed, but Eventing has so many roles for willing volunteers (indeed could not run without them) that an ambitious child who makes the grade, or indeed fails to, is no bar to becoming an integral part of the sport.

By definition it is an outdoor pursuit, more than often in a lovely location.

Here are some options:

• Score sheet runner: In the Enid Blyton days these were exclusively drawn from the local Pony Club, and at the top events still are. The duty is during the Cross Country section, when score sheets will need to be picked up from the judges at each fence and returned to the scorers' tent or HQ. This is a great, fun day out and more than one runner at Badminton has gone on to actually ride at the great event. Today, in the world of quad bikes and scramblers, local youth bike clubs take on the role. Provided there is strict safety monitoring this role provides a great day out for the young, especially if they are the potentially disaffected brother

of a 'horsey' sister.

• Jump judge: This responsible job increases with the level of competition and, indeed, the complexity of the obstacle that has been designated. The job is to tick a clearance of your obstacle or log any penalties incurred and note how they may have occurred if there should be a dispute. This role used to be a rather pleasant picnic outing for the more mature, where more than one Whisky Mac might be taken during the afternoon. The world has moved on, and clear responses are now regulation, but it is still a pleasant day out. The downside is that you are in the hot seat if a nasty fall happens. You will have back up.

• Radio operator: This is great fun for the 'over and out…Wilko Wilko… Charlie Charlie' fantasists. Usually the job is to report 'Fence 5…47 clear' or 'refusal'. If, however, there is an accident the radio operator has to report if the course needs closing and emergency services such as doctor, ambulance, vet or fence repair are needed to be scrambled. The radio operator reports to 'Control'.

• Control: This is the nerve centre of operations during the all important Cross Country section. Even at the most modest events, without TV monitors and high tech communications, Control is the main safety centre of the operation. Usually there will be a long, wooden peg board, owned and built by the itinerant controller (so they are all a bit different), which will have a masking tape strip with the names and numbers of each obstacle, and emergency stopping points, if the course needs to be closed. The controller will have two feeds to his headphones: one from the jump radio operator and the other to the emergency services. He (they really all seem to be men!) will plot the progress of each horse round the course, like the WRAF girls in WW2 movies. If there is a 'prang' the controller is in charge of getting the emergency services to the jump and making sure that the course is closed if necessary. With 175 fixtures a year there is a lot of control that goes on but not that many controllers. Control has a red/green traffic light control which will be linked to the start and no horse will go while the course is on Red.

• Commentators: commentators and announcers are the public voice of the event. In 170 of the 175 events they will have no audience! This has never been a problem, since the competitors and their connections are happy to hear the progress of their star, and the ambient, avuncular tones, give tone to the proceedings. The occasional *bon mot* is acceptable and 'in jokes' can be done, but wannabe comedians should be kept a million miles from the microphone. Clare Balding may be a national treasure, but on the whole PA microphones are unkind to the higher register voice. The big test can come when there is a hold up. The controller will be monitoring the situation, but total silence from the commentator can alert the spectators that something is amiss. Conversely, too much inane banter over the loudspeakers can be equally off putting.

• Control assistant: Cross Country control is the most interesting place to spend the day, as it is the nerve centre of the operation and where all the crisis management takes place. While the controller is boss and the commentator the 'voice', and indeed in many boxes there will be three people who rotate from commentator through control to hour break, there will be a team who hand the controller the next rider slip to

go on the plotting board, and then take them back at the end of the round. The assistant will be in phone contact with the start and finish who will state which horse is next, and the time of the latest finisher has been taken. The assistant will calculate the time penalties and sort current leaders into order, so that the commentator can give an instant state of play if there is time for a gap in the course chat.

• Dressage judge: Obviously some expertise is needed for this role and judges work their way up the rankings and up the level of events. It can be a long day, and at One Day Events the judge may be expected to sit through perhaps 60 tests. In Eventing any notion of Olympic level 'dancing horses' should be put aside. In the main the tests are very mundane, involving not much more than circles and straight lines at trot walk and canter, but there will always be something to mark.

• Judges' writer: This can be quite fun for someone who is wanting to get involved, but also wants to watch and learn. While the judge is pontificating, the writer will have a clip board with the test movements marked out with a box for the mark and a slot for the judges'

comments. These can run from the single word to acerbic sentence. The sheets are available for the riders to scrutinise at the end of play.

• Starter/finish: You are the 'Three, two, one, GO' person, normally installed in a caravan with electronic timing systems and back up stopwatches. If there has been a hold up the starter will want to try and make the time up by sending horses off at shorter intervals. This is where they can have a difference of opinion with the controller (who is senior!), as too many horses on the course can be a safety problem.

• Course designer: As with Dressage judges, obviously some knowledge is a necessity. Many of the best course designers have naturally been top riders themselves: Frank Weldon (Badminton), Mark Phillips (Burghley, Gatcombe), Hugh Thomas (Badminton, Seoul Olympics), Mike Etherington-Smith (Blenheim, Sydney and Hong Kong Olympics), Sue Benson (Bramham, Greenwich Olympics), though Burghley has had a vet in Bill Thompson and a clerk of the course in Philip Herbert. Newcomers at the top are Ian Stark (Bramham) and Eric

Winter (Blenheim). Obviously designers have to start somewhere and most start as understudies to an established designer. Again there is a ladder to climb. The course designer's job, even at the small events, holds the most responsibility for two reasons. The safety of the track is of paramount importance, but also it has to provide a result. Also the whole ambience of the event is designated by its course or courses. In modern years each event has a senior riders' representative, so if riders have a concern, changes will be made. In these days when safety is so important and has to be seen to be important, a course builder has the unenviable task of putting up a challenging track to thrill the spectators, but keeping it safe for horse and rider. In the past no one was too bothered if half the field of a major event failed to get round. Now it is very different. Of course the spectators would rather see horses at each jump without long gaps between competitors.

• Course builder: These are the boys with chainsaws, pickup trucks and calloused hands, who realise the ideas of the course designers. They are the artisans of the equestrian world and are in demand on an international level. Badminton's Willis Brothers have built courses all round the world, and for the Greenwich Olympics an enterprising gang of British builders created a consortium to create Sue Benson's masterpieces. The constrictions of Greenwich meant that the majority of jumps had to be made off site, and planted just before the competition, and by way of 'legacy' have been making guest appearances at other events round the country, including Badminton, Burghley and Blenheim.

• Steward: Stewards are the helpful souls who chivvy the riders into the ring or starting box. They must be quietly efficient and unflappable, but also possess a good, clear calling voice. All they want out of a day is to be thanked by riders.

• Event organiser (standard): This role is for the saints and masochists of the world. Several riders have gone on to run events under the auspices of 'putting something back'. In theory an event can make some money and several are run to raise funds for the local hunt or charity, however the vagaries of the British weather still make this a risk. There is a group of formidable ladies (usually) who run/secretary several events round the country. There are a couple of men in the field who run several: Alec Lochore who ran Greenwich and former Australian rider, Stuart Buntine, who attempted to fly the idea of off season indoor Eventing. They will have to deal with all the entries, organise and recruit volunteers, book emergency services of doctor, ambulance vet and course repair.

• Director (great events): These jobs are few and far between and are usually held for long stints by their incumbents. It was a male preserve, but in recent years Liz Inman has taken the helm at Burghley and Mandy Hervieu at Blenheim, each stepping up from the secretariat side of operations. With the big events real money can be made (or lost to weather!) and the responsibilities grow to include ticketing, crowd control, TV contracts, and today all the new forms of communications and social media.

• Press Officer: Even the smaller events can do with a bit of publicity, but much of this is helped by HQ at British Eventing, however, at the big events, where there will be a Press centre, they usually have someone who looks after press releases, accreditation, film crews, bibbing photographers. On some occasions the Press Officer will have to act as spokesman and go on the radio or TV if the director is unavailable.

• Press assistant: This is a fun job during a major event, since the assistants will be sorting passes for accredited journalists and photographers and calling up riders for interviews. There is always a buzz around a Media centre and usually there will be representatives from the major papers who will need looking after, as for many of the feature writers, this may be their first horse trial, and they will need a helpful hand if they are going to write nice things about the event.

• Lunch lady: At the regular events the volunteers need feeding and watering. Sometimes they are provided with a packed lunch at the beginning of the day, but sometimes there is a welcome lunch run. In the 'good old days' volunteers used to bring their own picnics, which contained a fair amount of liquid refreshment. After incidents of dozing jump judges, tighter rules now apply.

All events need this army of helpers, some experts in their field, others just a very welcome spare pair of hands.

Right: *Pony Club Runners*

You Can Do It

YOU CAN DO IT

Far Right: *Riding Clubs*

In the past most people who went Eventing did so because they had come from a 'horsey' family and had come up through the Pony Club. It has now opened up to a much wider participant group, as more mature riders take up the sport later on. There were always Riding Clubs, whose organisation have had their own championships, but more recently British Eventing has introduced a Grass Roots level of competition, which is open to children, older amateur riders and also established riders with their youngest horses. These mini jump test rides have taken on a life of their own and have turned out to be a great income source to the sport. Not only that, but they have recently held their own championships during the week of, and on the sacred turf of, Badminton.

In a strange twist the ultimate test including Roads and Tracks and Steeplechase is still retained at some of these mini events (though not at the Badminton finals). Those sections were fun and it is ironic that they no longer exist at the top end of the sport, but retain the ultimate aim at the lowest level of the sport.

These smaller competitions are greatly democratic, as all sorts of horses and ponies can compete on equal terms. For some reason, however, the riders at this level tend to go for the most exotic of Cross Country gear. In darkest history the British team strip was a black helmet

Right: *Camp*

silk and white polo neck sweater. Indeed, the Germans had a very similar team uniform. At Grass Roots competitions riders are decked out in multi-coloured stars, stripes, moons and quarters, and all helmet silks are set off with a furry bobble. Coloured breeches are also not unknown.

The well known model and Dressage participant, Katie Price, markets a

great range of pink jods and diamante encrusted riding boots. They are yet to be seen in the arena at Badminton and Burghley, but have certainly been at those venues for sale!

There is now a network of what is termed 'unaffiliated' which means the events aren't actually under the official auspices of the governing body, but are often run at the same sites as the official

events, with the same back up. It has become something of an ambition of weekend riders to go 'affiliated', and to qualify for the Grass Roots final.

A first time Eventer needs to make friends with someone who has done it before. The greatest thing about the sport is that at every rung of the ladder the people one rung up are happy to help, but better than that, the people at

the VERY top are happy to help as well.

In almost any other sport, the idea of a star being in the same vicinity of a novice is inconceivable.

Think of a golf hacker playing the same course and time as Tiger Woods; a banger racer up with Jenson Button; a garden party tennis player doing doubles with Andy Murray.

In Eventing this happens every day.

Right: *Grassroots*

LITTLE BOOK OF **EVENTING**

End Piece

Far Right: *Early Eventing*

Eventing has come a long way since those old cavalry tests, and in a world where the cavalry regiments moved to tanks, which in their turn have become redundant in modern warfare, the sport's origins shouldn't be forgotten.

The relative tests may have changed many times in the development, but these have been evolution not revolution. Eventing today, even without the endurance tests of old, and the sort of courses where only half the competitors expected to complete is still the ultimate test of the all-round rider. Even at the lower level riders have the privilege of galloping around someone's farm or park. At the top level vast crowds witness top class competition in some beautiful surroundings and there is some form of role for supporters old and young.

Eventing really is a sport that can be enjoyed from so many angles and by so many diverse people, despite, or perhaps because of its upmarket image, which is ironically very welcoming and inclusive.

Acknowledgements

Thanks are due to Kate Green, Paul Graham, Martin Renfrey and Winnie Murphy who checked the text for accuracy and to Rhydain Wynn-Williams, who compiled international statistics for many years. My published sources include *Horse and Hound* and *Eventing* magazines, *The Horseman's Year 1946-1947*, edited by W.E. Lyon, and *Porlock Vale Riding School 1946-1961* by Jacqueline Peck.

Right: *Crowds at the Festival of British Eventing, Gatcombe*

**The pictures in this book were provided
courtesy of the following:**

KIT HOUGHTON
WWW.HOUGHTONSHORSES.COM

Design and artwork by Scott Giarnese

Published by G2 Entertainment Limited

Publisher: Jules Gammond

Written by Julian Seaman

Dedication
This book is for Adrian 'Eggy' Ffooks.

Julian Seaman evented from the age of nine and was lucky enough to have ridden
at Badminton and Burghley. He has been on the board of the sport and written for
most equestrian magazines. He is Press Officer at Badminton and held the same
post at the Greenwich Olympics.